G000167912

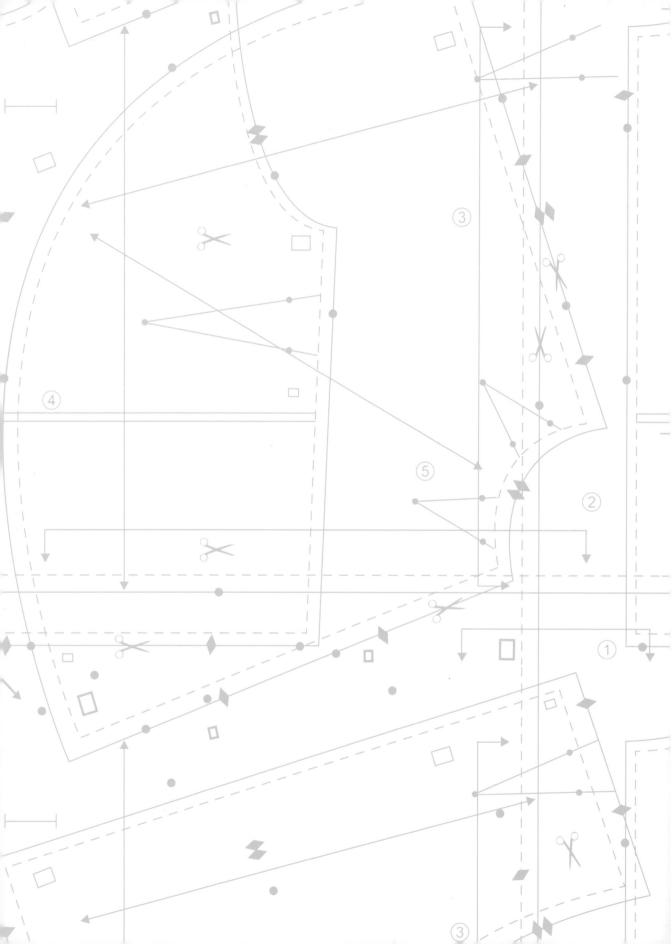

QUINTESSENTIALLY

GENTLE

MAN

ALFRED DUNHILL

ARCHER ADAMS

ASPINAL OF LONDON

CAD & THE DANDY

DALMORE

DASHING TWEEDS

DEGE & SKINNER

DENTS

ETTINGER

FIELDING & NICHOLSON

GIEVES & HAWKES

HENRY POOLE

HOLLAND & HOLLAND

JAEGER

JIMMY CHOO

JUST BLAZE

KILGOUR

LINKS OF LONDON

MR HARE

MULBERRY

MURDOCK LONDON

N.H SARTORIA

OLIVER PEOPLES

PASSAGGIO CRAVATTE

PAUL SMITH

RALPH LAUREN

RAY WARD

RICCARDO BESTETTI

SHARP & DAPPER

SHAW SPEED CUSTOM

TED BAKER

VILLA

QUINTESSENTIALLY

GENTLE

MAN

Contents

INTRODUCTION

THE ART OF BEING A GENTLEMAN
by Peter Archer

There is nothing old-fashioned or *passé* about being a gentleman. Etiquette may have changed with the times, but style and grooming remain the essence of who you are. A modern gentleman should be at ease in the world and know how to cut a dash. Making a good first impression is crucial. You may offer a firm handshake, but don't overlook making eye contact. Make others feel like they are the centre of attention.

But, of course, dress and behave in a way that sets you apart from the ordinary. Be noticed. However, strive to achieve an understated elegance.

A well-cut suit, which flatters, is essential. Do buy silk ties with a wool interlining. Flowers, stripes and bold colours are fine. Quality footwear is a must: remember it's brown for out of town. So dress for the occasion. Casual is OK, but create "your look" which should be considered and addressed with care. Whether you wear your hair long or short, get a good cut and know what suits your face. Hygiene goes without saying and always maintain a neat manicure. Work out and stay in trim. Love your body and others will love you.

But never forget: quintessentially, manners still maketh man.

"Good manners
will open doors that
the best education
cannot."

Clarence Thomas

CHAPTER ONE

The Brand

RALPH LAUREN

RALPH LAUREN

THE CUSTOM TRADITION: RALPH LAUREN'S MADE TO MEASURE RANGE

Utter the name Ralph Lauren and people with access to any kind of media information will think of the famous Polo logo. More than just a global name and logo though, Ralph Lauren – the brand – has, since its beginnings in 1967, defined a classic American fashion that has come to be one of the most sought-after and referenced on the planet.

We owe all the Ralph Lauren fashion collections we have today to the brand's first men's ties, the Polo Ralph Lauren collection, launched in 1967. Prior to this, Ralph Lauren himself had gained some experience working in menswear that stood him in good stead for his swift move into establishing his own fashion brand.

The famous Polo logo saw the light of day in Lauren's first line of suits for women, tailored in a classic men's style, at the end of the 1960s. It was around this time that business really took off with the opening of the first stand-alone Polo Ralph Lauren store in Beverley Hills.

← 1. RALPH LAUREN PURPLE LABEL MADE TO MEASURE - credit Nathan Copan · → 2. RALPH LAUREN PURPLE LABEL - credit Sheila Metzner · 3. RALPH LAUREN PURPLE LABEL - credit Martyn Thompson ·

Iconic short-sleeved mesh Polo shirts, which remain staple luxury items, followed in a vast range of vibrant colours and it wasn't long before the rest of the world succumbed to this powerhouse of fashion. Notwithstanding name and logo changes along the way, the RL story continues to be one of the most successful in fashion history to this day.

One prerequisite remains throughout the decades, however: to deliver an exquisite take on classic tailoring. Clients have come to rely on the enduring quality of the brand's clothing, from the simplest of Polo shirts to the finest evening suit, and have shifted into new territory since the 1990s, with the resurgence of traditional bespoke values in tailoring at Ralph Lauren.

As gentlemen's wardrobes accommodate a growing need for one-off timeless pieces, so naturally, the Made to Measure programme has set our pulses racing with its infinite possibilities. Choose from any of Ralph Lauren's clothing models, fine materials and fabrics, and you can have your custom-modified pattern made for you by master tailors in Italy. The Purple Label Sartorial Suit sits well under this bespoke umbrella and allows for limited-edition fabrics and yardage as well as a shorter waiting time for your finished item should you so desire.

What could be more rewarding than having a select group of artisans dedicated to overseeing the creation of your suit from beginning to end?

4

← 4. RALPH LAUREN MW ACCESSORIES - credit Martyn Thompson - → 5. 6. RALPH LAUREN PURPLE LABEL MADE TO MEASURE - credit Nathan Copan - 7. RALPH LAUREN PURPLE LABEL MADE TO MEASURE - credit Studio W26 - 8. RALPH LAUREN PURPLE LABEL MADE TO MEASURE - credit Martyn Thompson -

Picture the finest tweeds, the softest flannels and the most luxurious cashmere, swathed in colours as sumptuous and elegant as chocolate brown, midnight blue and deep burgundy, in cuts to suit the precise weight of the material and the wearer's silhouette; all complete with the inner silk lining in regal purple, of course.

No bespoke suit would be complete without the all-important accessories and the perfect shoes to tie your look together. Why not plump for the finest monogrammed shirt ordered through the online service or a pair of engraved silver cufflinks to achieve your personal style statement? You could be donning your hand-stitched bespoke RL Purple-look in less time than you think.

5

6

7

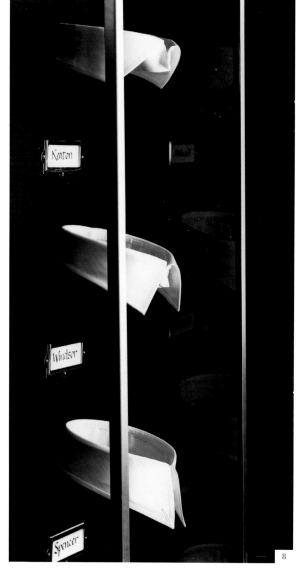

8

PAUL SMITH

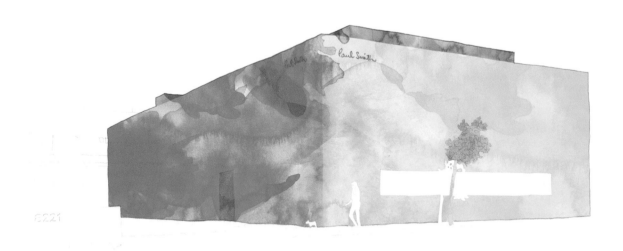

THE MAN BEHIND THE BRAND

A sense of humour is one of the most endearing qualities a
person can have. If you think about it, people who tell witty
stories and clever jokes are usually the most memorable.
The British pride themselves and place great store by this
particular trait. A natural flair for humour was exactly
what Paul Smith wanted to play on when he first set about
becoming a fashion designer in the 1960s.

Paul Smith's designs are classic on the outside and
unconventional on the inside. A brightly coloured lining or
mismatched buttons lend a gorgeous twist. Take his Taupe
Glen Check Jacket: it's a classic wool, checked jacket, but is
lined with a dark-blue and plum paisley pattern. It is these
unconventional subtleties that make Paul Smith's designs so
unique and so quintessentially British.

Born in Nottingham in 1946, Smith grew up with the
dream of becoming a racing cyclist. After a serious accident
on his bike, he was in hospital for six months when he

← 1. → 2. 3. PAUL SMITH CATWALK COLLECTION SPRING / SUMMER 13.

made some new friends. Once out of hospital, he met up with them for a drink and they struck up conversation with students from the local art college. They discussed the influential figures of the time – Warhol, David Bailey, Kokoschka, The Rolling Stones. It was then that Paul knew he wanted to be part of this exciting world of ideas. Within two years he was running his first boutique in Nottingham. With the help of his future wife, Pauline Denyer, and a small amount of savings, he opened his own, tiny shop in 1970. At first the shop was open just two days a week, and in his spare time the designer took classes in tailoring, using his knowledge to offer a bespoke service with every shirt he sold. Individualism was key.

Now, admirers of British fashion put Paul Smith at the top of their must-have list. The iconic logo, Smith's own signature, defines excellence and sophistication in the fashion world. Comprising 12 collections for men, women and children, Paul Smith designs are sold across five continents, with shops everywhere from Melbourne, Australia to Las Vegas's South Boulevard, and of course London and Nottingham too. Always keenly focused on the detail, each Paul Smith shop differs from the next, from a bright pink building with a movie set theme in LA, to a Japanese garden at the heart of the Jingumae store in Tokyo.

4/5

← 4. 5. → 6. 7. PAUL SMITH CATWALK COLLECTION SPRING / SUMMER 13

Famous for his clothing and accessories collections,
Paul Smith is known for his inventive use of traditional
craftsmanship combined with cutting-edge design. Staging
four international fashion shows each year, classic British
trends are given a twist of authenticity and originality.
Needless to say, the Quintessentially British Gentleman
should dress smart and confidently at all times. What better
way to incorporate wardrobe essentials with splashes of
colour and hand-finished detail than Paul Smith's menswear?

ALFRED DUNHILL

"IT IS NOT ENOUGH TO EXPECT A MAN TO PAY FOR THE BEST, YOU MUST ALSO GIVE HIM WHAT HE HAS PAID FOR..."

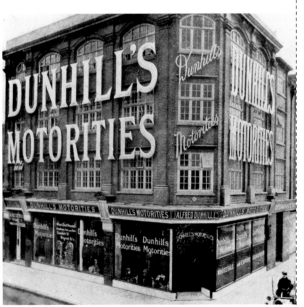

The name "dunhill" conjures up powerful notions of British tradition and style. The clothing and accessories embody elegance and illustrate a considerable creative intelligence and craftsmanship. All around us are traces of the dunhill legacy from snappy items like the first butane gas cigarette lighter, which was introduced by Alfred Dunhill in the mid-1950s and regularly features in James Bond stories, to the iconic Tradition leather briefcases entirely handmade in dunhill's London workshop.

We owe our most ingenious motor-car accessories to Alfred Dunhill too. When he took over the family saddlery business in 1893, this highly innovative man embarked upon one of the most creative adventures in Great Britain. Beyond the leather cricket and golf goods, the fishing rods and saddles, larger ideas were brewing.

To those who knew him, at the beginning of the 20th century, it was no surprise that he should own one of the first

← 1. ALFRED DUNHILL FIRST STORE - EUSTON ROAD → 2. ALFRED DUNHILL TAILORING IN WOOL TWILL 3. TRADITION LEATHER

motor cars in Britain. At the time, cars would come straight from the manufacturer with a chassis and an engine, and nothing else. Alfred felt compelled to provide "everything but the motor" to his customers in a line known as the "dunhill Motorities". It included leather driving coats and helmets, goggles, dashboard clocks and luggage trunks. He even brought us the car horn and the articulation of the rear view mirror in 1907, prompting him to set up his own Patent Development Company in 1908 to accommodate his weird and wonderful creations.

A first store in London in 1907 paved the way for openings in New York and Paris in the 1920s, leading to more than 20 stores around the world by the 1970s. Over the decades we have seen heritage, craftsmanship and innovation form the basis of all the dunhill collections.

Alfred Dunhill once said: "It is not enough to expect a man to pay for the best, you must also give him what he has paid for…" Today the brand clearly continues to embrace this promise to their consumers by quite literally going to the ends of the Earth to deliver collections that celebrate the finest materials and skills of the finest artisans – from supporting British cottage-industry weavers or Tokyo's generational lacquer artists, to working with local farmers to get the purest mohair from the mystical regions of Camdeboo in South Africa.

← 4. ALFRED DUNHILL EVENINGWEAR IN MOHAIR AND VELVET   → 5. BOURDON HOUSE, LONDON HOME OF ALFRED DUNHILL

The brand's most ambitious project to date has compounded this commitment with a series of exceptional retail Emporiums for men. The "Homes of Alfred Dunhill" as they are known, carefully create a "living experience of luxury" in which the customer can be fully immersed in the world of dunhill. The spiritual, flagship "Home" is in London's Mayfair at Bourdon House. This Grade II-listed Georgian building is an incredibly distinguished retail environment set out on three spacious levels that include a bespoke tailoring

service, a barber's shop, a humidor, a bar and restaurant, a screening room and a spa. The experience has been successfully translated to Shanghai, Tokyo and Hong Kong, and, were Alfred alive today, there's no doubt he would have approved of this exciting vision.

It's no secret that when you enter the circle of the dunhill gentleman, you're in excellent company. Patrons of the brand have included Frank Sinatra and Truman Capote, for whom

← 6. TWIN VILLAS, SHANGHAI HOME OF ALFRED DUNHILL

suits were cut and named in their honour. For Capote, it was a tuxedo that he wore to the glamorous Black and White Ball he hosted in 1966. The occasion proved to be a landmark in New York's high-society calendar and the suit itself was the very epitome of masculine elegance.

It would seem that influential and talented men have long been the collective muse of dunhill and never more so than in recent years. Since 2011, in a fascinating campaign of images and content entitled "Voice", shot as portraits and four-minute black-and-white vignettes, the viewer is privy to some of the most accomplished men expressing their deepest thoughts and aspirations. These telling films feature the likes of Don McCullin, John Hurt, Brian Eno and Sir Ranulph Fiennes to name but a few. They form an ingenious alliance that reflects a thoughtful brand with deep respect for the modern-day gentleman – the "thinking man".

→ 7. TRUMAN CAPOTE IN ALFRED DUNHILL AT THE BLACK AND WHITE BALL, 1966

TED BAKER

MAKING A STATEMENT WITHOUT EVER SAYING A WORD

Take a walk down all major shopping streets and you'll soon realise that Ted Baker is at the forefront of fashion – especially men's. It was the shy but utterly brilliant Ray Kelvin who founded this young company, opening the first store in Glasgow in 1988, specialising in men's shirts. Today Ted Baker's stock values continue to rise while many of its contemporaries have fallen by the wayside. So what is it that sets Ted Baker apart? With an eye for quirky details and a love of classic British style, the clothes and accessories tap into two fundamental requirements. They maintain their traditional values while staying well ahead of the fashion game. The result is a wildly successful brand that is popular with the modern, sophisticated gentleman.

Kelvin focused on faultless quality and built the company's reputation through word-of-mouth rather than advertising to spread the word. Indeed the fact that his first store offered free laundry services was not only a real

← 1. CLOCKWISE FROM TOP LEFT: CHARJACK, SAILSEE, LUPINN, ZABJAK, BURN ST, ANNKA, MIXTON, KENDO, KANPUR, VASHITA, PATMA, JAMERO, ROLANDO, LITERALL, SMLNICE, DORBEL, HARLEMM → 2. JACKET GATZBYT, WAISTCOAT GATZWAY, SHIRT GAR-B, TIE TIECHEK, POCKET SQUARE MRSPOT, TROUSER GATZBYT, SOCK MIXUD, SHOE CASSIUS. 3. JACKET ISLANDT, KNIT BOSKOPP, SHIRT GATSBEE, TIE ANNARC, POCKET SQUARE POURMIX, TROUSER ISLANDT, SOCK SHADOH AND SHOE CASSIUS

draw for regular clients, but allowed his name to travel like wildfire. Ten years later, Kelvin opened a store in the fashion hub of New York City and by 2007 had opened 11 new stores in the US. Kelvin's hard work paid off and he was awarded a CBE by the Queen for services to the fashion industry in 2011.

This quintessentially British brand embodies confidence and charm with v-neck sweaters, patterned ties and beautifully cut blazers. Purple button-down jackets embroidered with dogs and canine themed ornaments set the tone for the Christmas season of 2012 – following on from the Jubilee and Olympic celebrations.

The Ted Baker stores themselves are cleverly designed. Elegant chandeliers overhang immaculate racks and shelves of brightly assorted items in a vintage feel with a twist. Hand-painted, colourful dressers and tables display cuff links and accessories in a homely but artful way, and there are touches of regal purple and plush velvety textiles throughout the stores, making for a calming environment.

Kelvin didn't stop there though. Men are catching on to the virtues of grooming more than ever before and Ted's Grooming Room, of which there are four in London, offers the perfect hand-shave and sharp haircut. The service has fast become a firm favourite with Ted Baker customers.

4

← 4. JACKET FABZJ, WAISTCOAT ISWWAY, SHIRT GENERVA, TIE MARIARL, POCKET SQUARE SMLNICE, TROUSER FABZT AND SHOE CASSIUS. → 5. CLOCKWISE FROM TOP LEFT: HAT ATLANTE, JACKET ISLANDJ, TRAVEL WALLET ROLLAA, IPAD CASE THELINE, BAG CAVESON, WALLET JONCASH, HAT DEALES, SCARF BOATLET, IPAD TWEETEE, KINDLE WEFOLD, BAG SKOLDAY, BAG HARLEMM, BAG DREVIL, BAG DRSPOCK, WASHBAG DRBEAT, UMBRELLA LEROSS, BAG HILLTOP, BAG STOWELL, BAG DRUMLEN .6. THE PYRAMID PEEK POCKET SQUARE TECHNIQUE 7. FOURMIX POCKET SQUARE

Combining ancient techniques, used by the Ottoman Empire's master barbers, with the latest cutting-edge products, customers can book a full shave or haircut safe in the knowledge they're in good hands. Trust is highly prized at Ted Baker and nowhere is this more obvious than with the brand's loyal fan base. Men (and women) choose their wardrobe staples and seek advice from Ted Baker. In an age of uncertainty, a dependable brand such as this is a valuable asset and one which heralds a bright future – preferably punctuated with a little dash of purple for good measure.

5

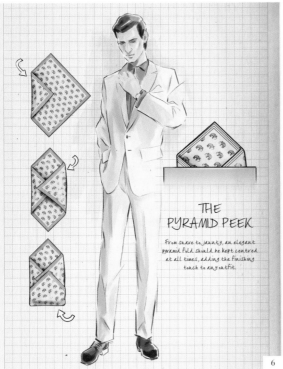

THE
PYRAMID PEEK

From suave to jaunty, an elegant
pyramid fold should be kept centred
at all times, adding the finishing
touch to any outfit.

6

7

JAEGER

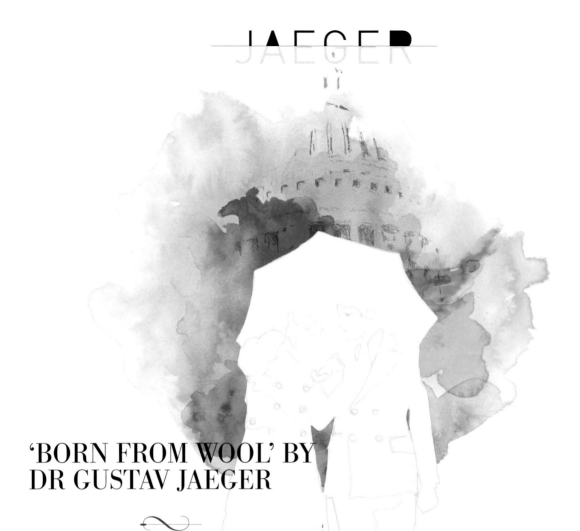

'BORN FROM WOOL' BY DR GUSTAV JAEGER

For the best part of a century, the name Jaeger has stood for sophisticated and hard-wearing high fashion. Jaeger's desirable merino woollen coats, cosy cashmere sweaters and tactile angora jackets have been a staple of the British fashion industry since the 1930's, but the story starts in 1884.

Dr Gustav Jaeger researched the health benefits of wearing animal fibres next to the skin; a fact we take for granted now, but which was groundbreaking at the time. Thankfully, Lewis Tomalin published a translated version of Jaeger's book on the subject, taking up the Jaeger mantle.

Flawless quality and durability worked beautifully with Jaeger's inventive fabrics, detail, cut and finish. Customers frequently boast of 30-year-old Jaeger pieces still in perfect condition to this day. It's interesting to note that Captain Scott equipped himself with Tomalin's woollen clothing for his expedition to Antarctica in 1910.

← 1. HOUNDSTOOTH JACKET JAEGER MENSWEAR AUTUMN/WINTER 1996 → 2. 100% WOOL SUIT JAEGER MENSWEAR SPRING/SUMMER 2011 3. SPRING/SUMMER 2013 BRITISH BLUE PLAINWEAVE WOOL SUIT. THIS SUIT IS WOVEN AND FINISHED IN THE UK

Tomalin developed his brand and, by 1930, it had transformed into a sophisticated fashion house. There followed innovative washable fabrics and era-defining designs in navy, black and beige, shot through with twists of vivid colour. Jaeger's British heritage, coupled with a sense of fun, allowed polka dots and flowers to sit alongside pin stripes and dog-tooth patterns.

The new Millennium saw the rise of Jaeger's striking menswear collection. The fashion house's modern identity was reinforced with memorable imagery.

The Jaeger man loves fashion-forward British design and traditional craftsmanship, and indeed 80 per cent of Jaeger's tailoring this season is woven and refined in the UK. In 2013 the spring/summer season showcased beautifully bright and elegant designs. Woven silks, linen summer jackets and Breton stripe sweaters worked their magic in smart blue, sunny yellow or aquamarine. Some original details included statement brass buttons, classic herringbone suits with subtle pink over-check and high-collared jackets. We particularly love the lanolin-finished suits that retain their shape and wear exceptionally well.

Watch out for the Union Jack symbol on pieces crafted in the UK – another endearing sign of Jaeger's ongoing support for British industry.

THE WEST END GENTLEMEN'S REQUISITES

JAMES SHERWOOD

London is unique in the pantheon of world style capitals. No other city, be it Paris, Milan, New York or Vienna, has so high a concentration of historic purveyors of luxury goods dedicated to men as the square mile covering Mayfair, Piccadilly and St James's. Despite the best efforts of the German Luftwaffe, unscrupulous property developers, avaricious landlords, changing fashions and the economic rollercoaster of boom and bust of late, these craftsmen of what are charmingly known as gentlemen's requisites, have not only survived, but thrive, the lucky few in their original premises that have remained relatively untouched for centuries.

Shops familiar to heroic Regency gentlemen, such as Lords Nelson and Byron, the Duke of Wellington or George "Beau" Brummell – the founding father of severe English elegance – still line St James's Street and Piccadilly: hatter James Lock & Co (established 1676), vintner Berry Bros & Rudd (1698), royal grocer Fortnum & Mason (1707) and bookseller Hatchard's (1797), to name a few. The famous bow window built on the façade of White's Club on St James's Street where Brummell and his "Body Dandiacal" would observe and mock the passing show of inadequate tailoring remains the royal box of London gentlemen's clubs.

A modern gentleman can be dressed from homburg to oxfords by the same historic firms patronised by the sybaritic King Edward VII, such as shoemaker John Lobb Ltd (established 1866), gunsmith Purdey (1814) and antique jeweller Hancocks (1860), who all held the King's royal warrant, and enjoyed the patronage of Edward VII's grandson the Duke of Windsor. Similarly, you could follow the present Prince of Wales to his shirtmaker, Turnbull & Asser (1885), his perfumer Penhaligon's (1870) or his tailor Anderson & Sheppard (1906).

The makers of gentlemen's requisites were, and still are, essential to a gentleman's success in town. The lowly born Beau Brummell's exquisite taste earned him the friendship of the Prince Regent (later King George IV). Brummell understood that sartorial luxury is a need – a necessity – and the correct tailor, city shoe, woven silk tie, handmade shirt, fountain pen or writing paper are as important to a London gentleman-dandy today as technological requisites such as the Apple iPad or the BlackBerry.

The term "requisite" might seem at odds with the concept of a luxury. The Oxford English Dictionary defines "luxury" as "the habitual use of, or indulgence in, what is choice or costly,

→ 1. CIGAR BANDS WERE FIRST PRODUCED BY DUTCH IMMIGRANT GUSTAVE
BLOCK, WHO OWNED A CIGAR FACTORY IN HAVANA, IN THE 1830S. 2. BRONZE
SCULPTURE OF GEORGE 'BEAU' BRUMMELL BY IRENA SEDLECKA UNVEILED BY
PRINCESS MICHAEL OF KENT IN 2002 ON JERMYN STREET. 3. A BOX OF PURE
GOLD TIPPED CIGARETTES, PRODUCED BY ROBERT LEWIS IN THE 1920S, BEARS
THE CREST OF ONE OF THE HOUSE'S MOST LOYAL CUSTOMERS, THE PRINCE
OF WALES THE FUTURE KING EDWARD VIII. 4. THE INLAID WALNUT HUMIDOR
MADE BY ROBERT LEWIS FOR THE PRINCE OF WALES, CIRCA 1925.

whether food, dress, furniture or appliances of any kind". The goods handcrafted by the heritage houses of London's West End are undeniably choice and costly. But to a London gentleman they are not so much an indulgence, as the weapons necessary to conquer society. Clothes and accessories don't so much make the man, but exquisite attire signifies a degree of self-control, an understanding of refinement, and social and financial success.

In the language of male attire, the sculpted upper of a bespoke black oxford handmade shoe at John Lobb is as identifiable to fellow Lobb men as a Chippendale dining chair to an antiques expert. Similarly, the richness and density of a Turnbull & Asser seven-fold woven silk tie is to connoisseurs as easily spotted as the Garrick's salmon-and-cucumber stripe club tie.

Perfume, that most potent olfactory semaphore, says much about the man, particularly if, like Penhaligon's Hammam Bouquet, it has served as the scent of the Jermyn Street gent since 1872.

The benefit of trading over a hundred years is that a business has simply seen it all before. Financial power may cross continents within decades, but the gentlemen's requisites houses will always attract the attention of money, however new. The allure of "Handmade in England" – the high-water mark of craftsmanship – remains undimmed despite the terminal decline of British manufacturing since the Second World War. We are no longer a nation of craftsmen and shopkeepers. London firms who have traded for over a century are rare; those who make by hand on the premises have thus become national treasures.

Shoes are still made above or below the shop floor at John Lobb, Foster & Son, Cleverley and Trickers. Shirts are still cut at Budd in the Piccadilly Arcade, Turnbull & Asser and Hilditch & Key. Jewels are still set on the premises of Garrard, Asprey and Bentley & Skinner. Making a product bespoken by a gentleman is still the preserve of London's West End, and a craft to take great pride in and protect.

Certain streets in the West End remain a haven of civilised behaviour where, in the words of Wilde, if a gentleman can't be a work of art, he can wear a work of art crafted in Mayfair, Piccadilly and St James's. These streets are deeply saturated with the DNA of quintessentially British elegance, civility. A pleasure-seeking chap with epicurean taste can still chase the shadows of the Prince Regent, Mr Brummell, the Count d'Orsay, Edward VII, the Duke of Windsor, Cary Grant, Prince Charles and, as of 2011, the dashing Duke of Cambridge and Prince Harry, in search of the sublime as made by the superb.

London continues to offer discreetly chic addresses that will not bow to the mediocre. Luxury has indeed returned to the concept of "bespoken". There is something inherently honourable about a heritage firm that has nothing to recommend its services over and above a prestigious list of patrons that speaks for itself. Looking into a crystal ball, it does not take a Nostradamus to predict that the perfect gentleman, who is socially and financially successful, will consider his time the most precious commodity. If a captain of his industry has time to order a suit, choose a tie silk pattern or bespeak a shoe that takes no less than three months to complete, then he is declaring that he has earned the right to live like a Regency buck. There is no one more impoverished than the man who is a slave to his schedule.

We live in an age when every year a new Russian oligarch can become a major player on London's luxury goods landscape. Who is better equipped to meet the needs they never anticipated than firms who have traded for over a century, stood their ground and smuggled their reputation into a world that should consider them obsolete? The finest things in life take time to craft, no matter how many billions you have in the bank. History cannot be shrugged on like a fur coat, however many times a company seeks to assume such a weight of responsibility: London's landlords and property developers have to understand that heritage brands have earned the right to be preserved, protected and treasured.

The Perfect Gentleman: The Pursuit of Timeless Elegance & Style in London by James Sherwood is published by Thames & Hudson.

CHAPTER TWO

Bespoke

FOUNDERS OF
SAVILE ROW

Few who pass through Savile Row will know of its origins and that they date back to the establishment of Henry Poole & Co, the quintessential family business. This firm laid the foundations of Britain's first bespoke tailoring company when James Poole left his native Shropshire in 1806 to start a new life in London and set up a linen drapers shop in Everett Street, Brunswick Square.

A twist of fate brought James Poole to tailoring during the period of the Battle of Waterloo. He had begun to make tunics for Napoleon whose Volunteer Corps regiment was required to provide its own equipment. James and his wife Mary, though inexperienced at the time, produced such well-stitched tunics that they soon found themselves inundated with orders and subsequently set up as a military tailoring service.

Success continued and led to James Poole opening his own Regent Street emporium in 1822, later establishing

← 1. HENRY POOLE & CO, NUMBERS 36-39 SAVILE ROW (1846-1961) ORIGINALLY NUMBER 32 BUT SHORTLY AFTER HENRY MOVED IN THE WHOLE OF SAVILE ROW WAS RENUMBERED → 2. THE CLASSIC HENRY POOLE & CO DINNER JACKET 3. THE HENRY POOLE & CO SHOWROOM AT 15 SAVILE ROW

headquarters at 4 Old Burlington Street adjacent to Savile Row.

When he passed away in 1846, his visionary son Henry had great ambitions. He made the premises more spacious and added a palatial showroom to cater for a growing and discerning clientele. The new entrance opened on to the adjoining street of Savile Row and so began the story of the Savile Row suit.

Henry proved to be an astute businessman. Indeed by the time he died 30 years later, in 1876, he had attracted nearly every European monarch on to his books. His style epitomised a blend of British elegance and class, and as a result Henry Poole & Co became the most sought-after tailor in the Western world.

The family work ethic lived on through Henry's cousin Sam Cundey, who opened shops in Paris, Vienna and Berlin, and who by the early-1900s was employing 300 tailors and 14 cutters – a hitherto unprecedented tailoring achievement.

Perhaps most impressive of all – aside from quality of craftsmanship and two royal warrants from Queen Victoria and the present Queen Elizabeth II – is the sheer variety of cloths available for bespoke suits. You can select from more

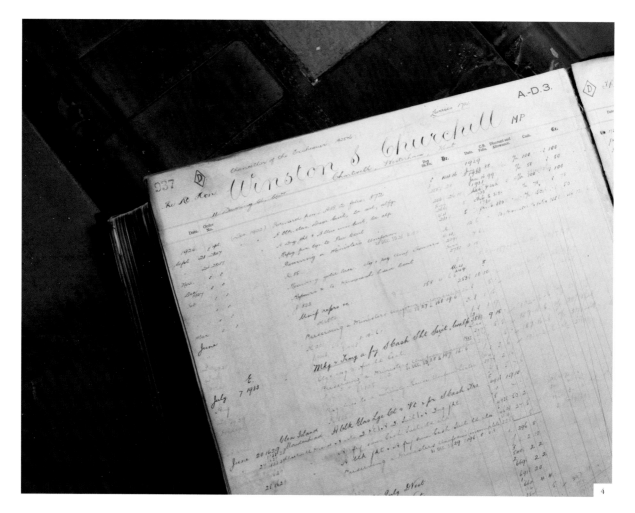

4

← 4. SIR WINSTON CHURCHILL'S ORDER ENTRIES ON HENRY POOLE & CO'S HISTORIC LEDGERS. HIS FIRST ORDER WAS PLACED IN 1905 → 5. HENRY POOLE & CO CLASSIC MIDNIGHT BLUE SILK VELVET SMOKING JACKET 6. HENRY POOLE & CO SHOP FRONT AT NIGHT (GOODWOOD WINDOW DISPLAY) 7. HENRY POOLE & CO WALKING GROOMS STATE LIVERY 8. HENRY POOLE & CO CLASSIC LAMBS WOOL ANGORA SPORTS JACKET

than 6,000 swatches that include luxury worsted cashmere from Yorkshire mills, sumptuous green West Country flannels and the finest Scottish tweed.

Clients are encouraged to visit the showroom and to complete their "look" with the all-important finishing touches – colourful ties, original cufflinks, braces and belts. All pieces are cut and stitched on the premises, though this doesn't deter a huge following from European customers, as well as further afield in America, Japan and the Middle East.

Great pride is taken to achieve a fully hand-finished garment made from natural materials that will stand the test of time. It's a meticulous process that is followed up with thoughtful after-sales care to allow for changes and alterations should a client's weight vary, for example.

Apprentices at Henry Poole & Co are nurtured through programmes that observe the traditional values of tailoring, in keeping with the founders' beliefs. Tailors also make regular visits around the world to service overseas clients, and senior cutters will frequently visit Europe to share developments.

5

6

7

8

DEFINING BRITISH ELEGANCE SINCE 1771

Savile Row – arguably the most important tailoring district in the world. It takes hard work and luck to secure your patch on this illustrious London street. It's fair to say that Gieves & Hawkes has a head start on the rest – situated at No1 Savile Row, though not without merit.

The story, of which there are two parts, charts a privileged relationship with the British military, navy and Royal Family. Thomas Hawkes set up his first tailor's shop in London's Brewer Street in 1771, where he serviced mainly commanders of the British Army, royal dukes and King George III. Hawkes' business grew along with his reputation and eventually earned him recognition with a number of royal warrants.

Elsewhere, in Portsmouth at the later date of 1852, James Gieve had partnered with a tailor supplying the Royal Navy and who famously dressed Lord Nelson for the fateful Battle of Trafalgar. By the time Gieve himself died in 1888, he had created a thriving company, Gieve and Company, leaving behind a tidy

← 1. A MODERN TWIST ON OUR FORMALWEAR OFFERING INCLUDES A MIDNIGHT BLUE DINNER SUIT → 2. A BESPOKE PRINCE OF WALES CHECK SUIT WITH CONTRAST STITCHING BUTTONHOLE 3. OUR SPRING/SUMMER '13 CAMPAIGN SHOWS A CASUAL TAKE WITH ELEGANCE

legacy. Indeed by the beginning of the 20th century, his company was the default supplier of British Navy uniforms.

Gieves & Hawkes' clientele reads like a Who's Who of the world's most influential figures – the present Duke of Cambridge, Charlie Chaplin, Bill Clinton, David Beckham and Mikhail Gorbachev, for starters. One glance at the bustling store with workshops, military archives, dashing garments, and impeccable service and craftsmanship will explain why.

If you're seeking a bespoke experience, venture to the store's grandiose address at No1 Savile Row and book a consultation with a bespoke tailoring adviser. You're assigned an experienced cutter (often attended by an under-cutter), who will consider the garment in relation to your physical build. The ensuing work is entirely hand-crafted. Over a period of eight to twelve weeks, your garment will go through "bastes" or creation processes, punctuated by at least three fittings, before the finishing touches are administered – edge stitching, individual buttonholes, pocket reinforcements and so on. After-sales service – freshening, brushing, repairing – on the finished garment will be as flawless as you'd expect from an internationally respected tailor.

For a more modest consideration, there is the recently launched Private Tailoring service. With more than 2,000 cloths in various styles and patterns to choose from for suits,

4

← 4. BESPOKE TAILORING IS THE SOUL OF GIEVES & HAWKES, WHERE EVERY STITCH AND DETAIL ARE MADE BY HAND BY SKILLED CRAFTSMEN → 5. DETAIL OF CAVALRY TUNIC [MADE CA. 1912], ORIGINALLY BELONGED TO EARL SPENCER. 6. A SNAPSHOT OF OUR CUTTING ROOM IN NO. 1 SAVILE ROW. 7. FAITHFUL CLIENTS INCLUDE THE GREAT AND THE GOOD OF BRITISH HISTORY. 8. DETAIL OF GREY BESPOKE JACKET IN HOPSACK CLOTH

coats and shirts, you are able to customise your wardrobe and make it stand out from the crowd with little details such as buttonholes and contrasted coloured stitching for the cuffs. The process will take six to eight weeks and is a must if you don't have the time for bespoke fittings.

The company's ready-to-wear offering focuses on seasonal specialities such as linen and cotton suiting for summer, and luxurious cashmere knitwear and outerwear for winter, not forgetting contemporary classics, namely the navy blazer, inspired by the company's naval history. With a huge range of

ties, handkerchiefs and accessories to complete the look, Gieves & Hawkes guides the sartorially minded gentlemen through the best of British menswear.

Mention you are a Quintessentially member at No. 1 Savile Row and rest assured you will get the finest service.

5

6

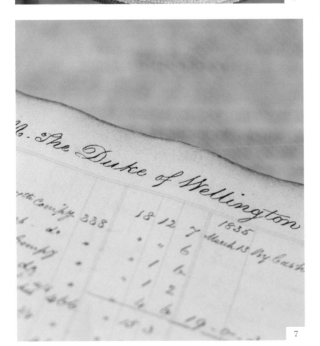

7

8

DEGE & SKINNER

SAFEGUARDING THE FUTURE OF TRADITIONAL TAILORING SKILLS ON SAVILE ROW

Savile Row is, without the shadow of a doubt, the most prestigious location in the bespoke tailoring world. To this day, there are select tailors here who produce bespoke clothing entirely from within their premises. That Dege & Skinner should be one such company speaks volumes about its passion to stay true to its original values. Dege & Skinner is also one of the few remaining family-run companies on Savile Row and prides itself on meticulous service: its tailors dedicate a minimum of 60 man-hours to produce a single three-piece bespoke suit.

From its beginnings in 1865, the company set out to clothe gentlemen in the finest military and sporting attire. The business thrived, visitors swiftly became faithful clients and royalty came knocking. Indeed, Dege & Skinner boasts three Royal Warrants to date. When Westminster Abbey hosted the 1953 Queen's Coronation Festival, the peers of the realm were proudly kitted out by Michael Skinner and John Dege. More recently, weekly fittings at

← 1. MESS KIT, QUEEN'S ROYAL LANCERS → 2. MASTER SHIRT CUTTER ROBERT WHITTAKER AT WORK, NUMBER 10 SAVILE ROW. 3. 3-PIECE NAVY HERRINGBONE BESPOKE BUSINESS SUIT BY DEGE & SKINNER

Sandhurst preceded the provision of full regalia for Prince William and Prince Harry on their commission with the Blues and Royals.

Dege & Skinner have consistently delivered the highest standards of bespoke tailoring but, perhaps more importantly, they enjoy an extraordinary loyal customer base. It's not surprising that some customers have been coming to shirt cutter Robert Whittaker for their bespoke pieces for over three decades. Clearly, the personal approach that comes so naturally to managing director William Skinner and his family business has paved the way for the next generation of sartorially savvy gentlemen.

PAUL SMITH
WESTBOURNE HOUSE

A LITTLE PIECE OF SAVILE ROW IN NOTTING HILL, PAUL SMITH BESPOKE TAILORING

They say every cloud has a silver lining and, in this case, the saying couldn't be more appropriate. After an accident prevented Paul Smith from pursuing his dreams of becoming a professional cyclist, he got a second chance to shine, this time in the world of fashion.

Paul Smith is now one of Britain's foremost designers, renowned for his creative spirit, which combines tradition and modernity. Famous for clothing and accessories collections, Paul Smith specialises in an inventive use of traditional craftsmanship and cutting-edge design.

With an enthusiasm for eclectic cultural references and idiosyncratic combinations of pattern and colour, applied with understatement, Paul Smith expresses a truly contemporary aesthetic. Beyond the impeccable suits and jackets, knitwear, shirting, garments and accessories, there is also a comprehensive bespoke service.

← 1. BESPOKE TAILORING → 2. A SELECTION OF BUTTONS AVAILABLE AT WESTBOURNE HOUSE 3. COLOUR SWATCH CARD

Paul Smith has been a fan of bespoke since the age of 17, when he befriended a tailor, Mr Hill, in his hometown of Nottingham. Paul would spend hours with the tailor, observing his work in progress. From the age of 21, when Paul met his now wife Pauline, his interest in tailoring began to develop, thanks in great part to her fashion training at the Royal College of Art. This was at a time when couture was still a vibrant sector and the art of clothes-making was of paramount importance. Paul would go to lots of couture shows in Paris in his early-20s, an experience that deeply influenced his love of tailoring. He had always dreamt about having a bespoke shop; a dream that he subsequently went on to fulfil.

At Paul Smith Westbourne House, the private Gurston Room, located on the top floor, is dedicated to tailoring of the highest standard, in both construction and technique. The team of ex-Savile Row tailors offers bespoke customers the opportunity to select from a wide choice of fabrics, English, Italian, and Scottish tweeds. There is also a

4

5

← 4. BESPOKE LABELS → 5. SIR PAUL SMITH

selection of fabrics that are unique and exclusive to the company.

An expert cutter will take the client's measurements and cut the pattern for a template garment to the exact shape of the customer's body. He then follows through its development in subsequent fittings until the customer is perfectly satisfied. The production of the suit will normally take between six and eight weeks, with two fittings and then completion.

The Paul Smith tailors work with the customer on their preferred style, cut and detailing. Colourful linings, embroidered detailing and hand-stitching mean that the

signature piece can be as discreet or flamboyant as the customer wishes.

KILGOUR

BESPOKE TRADITION, CONTEMPORARY DESIGN

What could Cary Grant, Fred Astaire and Jude Law possibly have in common? Apart from their celebrity, they also share a flair for dashing elegance, and have all at some point shared the same tailor – Kilgour.

There is a lot to be said for finding a tailor to whom you can entrust your bespoke wardrobe. And Kilgour, one of the oldest-established tailors on Savile Row, is no stranger to this calibre of gentleman. The most stylish men in the world have been coming to the shop premises since as far back as 1882 when it first opened.

The reason is deceptively simple – Kilgour provides a bespoke service that allows men to have their suits, jackets and shirts custom-made, from the first stitch to the final button. It also takes its services around the world for those based abroad.

In 2013, Kilgour looks set to add Africa and the Middle East to their trunk-show itinerary, which is already hugely popular

← 1. KILGOUR SIGNATURE HANDMADE READY TO WEAR 3 PIECE SUIT
→ 2. KILGOUR BESPOKE SILHOUETTE: FIRM SHOULDER, FULL CHEST AND AN
ELEGANTLY SUPPRESSED WAIST

in New York. Every few months, assigned teams of Savile Row tailors hold consultations with their overseas clients, accompanying them until the end of the cutting and fitting process.

While instilling a feeling of loyalty, the service also highlights the importance of the close, ongoing relationship between tailor and client. Every garment is cut, produced and basted entirely at Kilgour's premises. If you're lucky, you can catch a glimpse from the street of the tailors and seamstresses hard at work at their benches below.

ENGINEERED FOR LIVING, TAILORED FOR LIFE

Fielding & Nicholson have made quite a splash with their excellent tailoring consultations during which you'll be assigned a tailor to manage the meticulous process from start to finish. Any gentleman who has had the pleasure of wearing a bespoke garment and a good pair of shoes will tell you how a perfect fit can enhance the way you move and feel beyond imagination. To achieve such good results, Fielding & Nicholson have made it a mission to make the client feel as relaxed as possible. That's why the experts can also come to your office or home to complete the measuring and fitting process.

The materials used are top-notch and they proudly champion British craftsmanship. Particularly stunning are the variety of sumptuous wools spun in Yorkshire mills that work superbly with the suit cut – from 100-grade thread for chilly winter days to 220-grade thread for our elusive summers. All good things come to those who wait: several fittings and weeks later, you have a garment that

not only moves with your own body shape, but Fielding
& Nicholson can guarantee each bespoke piece for life.
For after-sales care, there are some precious handmade
accessories in-store that we highly recommend. Devised to
maintain and brush your suits with the utmost delicacy,
Amanda Christianson's accessories are handsome to boot,
adorned with luxury silks and brilliant silver. You can also
select from an impressive range of ties, pocket squares,
handkerchiefs and cufflinks.

CAD & THE DANDY

"STYLE IS A CHOICE, PRECISION IS AN ART, CONSTRUCTION IS A CRAFT."

Sometimes a breath of fresh air is just what's needed to whip the world of high fashion back into shape and inject a dose of healthy competition into proceedings. Currently causing ripples on London's bespoke tailoring scene is Cad & The Dandy, an ultra-sharp bespoke tailor that, somewhat refreshingly, believes its services should not be reserved for the lucky few. Indeed, the company subscribes to the idea that every gentleman should be able to stand proud in a handmade suit that celebrates quintessentially elegant British style.

James Sleater and Ian Meiers, who continue to lead the New Bespoke Movement, founded the discerning Cad & The Dandy in 2008. They shared a creative spark and set up their own business to expand on their passion for beautifully cut suits — and beautiful they are. Three grades of tailored suits are available: machine-stitched; half hand-stitched; and fully hand-stitched.

This exciting young company has taken Savile Row by storm with its team of on-site tailors and an arrestingly original range

← 1. EFFORTLESSLY COOL → 2. QUINTESSENTIALLY DANDY 3. 'BLENDING HERITAGE WITH MODERN'

of materials. If you crave the elegance and distinctive fit of a contemporary bespoke suit, without sacrificing any traditional construction elements, Cad & The Dandy is just the ticket.

Ordering one of these stunning suits is simple thanks to the company's modern and accessible approach. Appointments can be made across London in their shops – prepare for impeccable treatment – or clients can simply reorder online using an interactive design tool. The selection process is great fun with hundreds of design permutations, a vast library of fabrics and linings to suit your personality. All suits start with pattern creation, done by hand and retained for future orders, of which we suspect there will be countless.

NOBIL HOMO: SIMPLY ITALIAN CHIC

When it comes to a sleek finish, a handmade bespoke suit will run hoops around its comparatively run-of-the-mill, prêt-à-porter cousin. To the well-versed suit wearer, it's as simple as that.

Yet this is no simple business; you can be sure that the more the style and stitching appear effortless, the more painstaking the task becomes. Step aside for N.H Sartoria (the initials stand for Nobil Homo or Noble Man); a company with an enviable reputation for bespoke tailoring in its native Italy and among a global gathering of loyal followers.

Where else but Milan, one of the most influential fashion capitals in the world, for this tailor and his workshop to be based? One-to-one appointments at N.H Sartoria, during which clients can plan their entire 'trousseau', are legendary. The setting is the company's welcoming workshop adorned with plush fabrics and accessories that fire the imagination.

← 1. ULSTER COAT IN CASENTINO FABRIC → 2. MIDNIGHT BLUE SINGLE BREASTED SMOKING 3. N.H SARTORIA - MILAN ATELIER

For the uninitiated, a gentleman's trousseau is limited only by the imagination and can include shirts, ties and shoes, and new or vintage cufflinks featuring precious stones.

Let's come to the meat of the matter though - those beautiful suits, so expertly cut from the finest Italian and English fabrics.

When the successful owner of N.H Sartoria, Count Federico Ceschi a Santa Croce, met the renowned master tailor, Domenico Bombino, creative sparks flew. Federico Ceschi's career in fashion had nurtured a taste for masculine elegance, which he felt could only correctly be achieved with a customised fit. Bombino was of the same conviction and they joined forces to open their first workshop in 2003.

So what is the secret to N.H Sartoria's success? The philosophy and methods are exquisitely original and fashioned with care. The belief is that jackets should form naturally on the body, without requiring internal structures that often stiffen a look. The use of old artisan tradition is enhanced with unique sets of details, often hidden, that accentuate the wearer's personality and style like a fingerprint. No slavish trend following here. There is plenty of room however for gold, signature belt buckles and beautiful plaid pocket squares to reflect personal preference.

← 4. TIGHT OR MORNING SUIT 5. DOUBLE BREASTED NAVY BLAZER WITH
GOLDEN BUTTONS AND GOLF CLUBS TIE → 6. BASTED MIDNIGHT BLUE
SMOKING JACKET READY FOR THE FITTINGS 7. AMBER ON SILVER CUFFLINKS
(RUSSIA 1920) 8. FRONT PANTS BUTTON FLY

If you are looking for a cashmere jacket to wear on a chilly
winter's day, a green velvet tie, a navy blazer or a pinstriped
suit for the office, N.H can make virtually anything to fit
your needs. Aside from classic businessmen, the company's
Red Label caters for those with less time and money without
skimping on quality. So tell your sons and friends, young
entrepreneurs and professionals, who are just getting started,
that style need not elude them.

Count Ceschi would have it no other way and knows what
it is to start out with nothing and try to build something
special. He naturally epitomises his classy brand, without a
whiff of elitism, with his iconic wide-framed glasses, vibrant
ties and immaculate suits.

Above all, N.H makes gentlemen forget that they are
wearing a jacket and tie. And what could be nicer than that?

6

7

8

ARCHER ADAMS

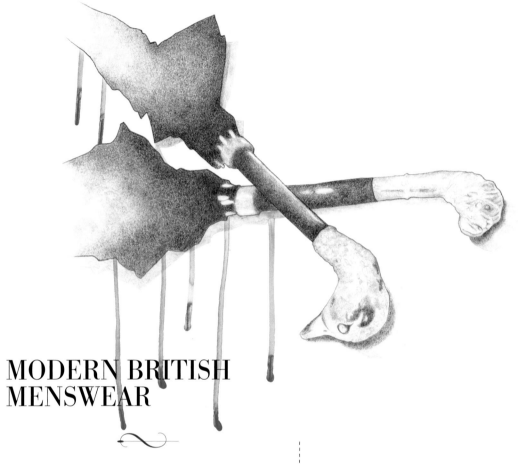

MODERN BRITISH
MENSWEAR

In a snug studio in London's fashionable Marylebone, Archer Adams stitches made-to-measure items along with in-store and online exclusives.

Launched in 2010, this up-and-coming boutique houses some eclectic and unique signature creations, as well as other groundbreaking fashion designs. Browse through the racks and you'll come across some real gems. They're picked for their fashion-forward styles and they blend in well with Archer Adams' own collections. There is something for every occasion so you can just as easily find the perfect evening jacket, unisex top or original form-fitting working suit.

Archer Adams' canny partnership with Portland General Store, means that clients can sample the delights of the latter's rustic Tobacco or Whiskey Cologne, Alpine Shaving Jelly or the ingenious vegan Thick Shampoo. The most popular items, however, have been Archer Adams' very own dignified silver-plated umbrellas and chauffeur hats crafted

← 1. ARCHER ADAMS OXFORD CLOTH SHIRT WITH SILK EDGING → 2. ARCHER ADAMS LONDON FLAGSHIP STORE IN MARYLEBONE W1

from colourful rigid Venetian wool. These pieces have earned some rave reviews in countless publications, bringing with them a newfound star status after only two years. Not a small task in any case and certainly not easy to maintain in a world that worships instant fame.

Don't be fooled though as there's far more to Archer Adams than meets the eye. Aside from the natural ability to mix and match across brands for the best results, the company's tailoring expertise is what really gets us excited. With highly personable service and meticulous attention to detail and styling, the fabrics and hand-stitched creations speak for themselves. Pick from the finest British and Italian velvets,

wools, selvedge denim and silk for your bespoke garment, and you'll be setting a guaranteed trend.

BRINGING TRADITIONAL SPORTSWEAR TO THE 21ST CENTURY

Dashing Tweeds is Britain's most recent tweed textile company that certainly lives up to its name.

It has positively breathed new life into this most traditional of fabrics, with its blend of contemporary designs. The result is quite a coup as it manages to bring a conservative, centuries-old textile crashing straight into 21st-century urban life with great aplomb.

Founders Guy Hills and Kirsty McDougall do have their share of industry experience. Guy, a successful photographer for many years, had become "fed up with marketing other peoples' designs" in a role that was "essentially a salesperson for brands". He felt increasingly compelled to create and sell his own designs. Kirsty was an established and exceptionally talented woven textile designer, with over ten years' experience, and the Jerwood and Testprint Prizes to her name. The pair met in 2007, at the Royal College of Art, when Kirsty clinched an opportunity to weave some fabric

← 1. SUIT IN SHFTI AND JIG BY DAVIES AND SONS SAVILE ROW. A BEAUTIFUL CLOTH FROM BRITISH SHFTI AND YARNS INSPIRED BY BAUHAUS GRAPHIC PATTERNS. A KNOCK ABOUT TWEED SUIT FOR ANY OCCASION. → 2. SUIT IN BLACK BASKET DESIGN TAILORED BY GRAHAM BROWNE AND PERFECT FOR AN EVENING ON THE TILES. 3. SUIT IN STEEL VIBE TAILORED BY HUNTSMAN, SAVILE ROW. SHAWL COLLAR AND CUT INSPIRED BY THE STYLE OF LEGENDARY 60'S POP GROUPS.

for Guy. It was at this point that Dashing Tweeds began to germinate as an idea between them.

The mere mention of tweed will inevitably conjure up visions of country folk, thatched cottages and picket fences. Not so for Guy. He and Kirsty love to draw their inspiration from seemingly contradictory art forms, notably Vivienne Westwood's fashion and the early punk scene. Rather than see tweed as limiting, this dynamic duo thrives on broadening its possibilities for design and its weavability.

Guy's passion for cycling sparked the idea of weaving reflective yarn into urban tweeds. Forget the embarrassment of turning up to a business meeting lit up like a Christmas tree in head-to-toe neon gear, not to mention the dreaded clothes-change pit stop in a freezing office. Why not just sport a striking tweed suit you can actually cycle in and be done with it? Dashing Tweeds certainly cater for the urban lifestyle with many patterns and designs even incorporating a weave to represent double yellow lines and tyre marks.

4

← 4. THE NEW WAVE SUMMER TWEED TAILORED BY DAVIES AND SONS SAVILE ROW INSPIRED BY EDWARDIAN SCHOOL UNIFORM → 5. SUIT IN CENTRE POINT PART OF OUR URBAN BLOCK SERIES TAILORED BY HUNTSMAN. THE CUT IS BASED ON 'WHITE TIE TAILS WITH THE TAIL CUT OFF' 6. THE MCDOUGALL CHECK, OUR TAKE ON THE CLASSIC GLEN URQUHART CHECK AND TAILORED BY HENRY POOLE SAVILE ROW 7. A FROCK COAT TAILORED BY CONNOCK AND LOCKIE IN THE FISHER DESIGN 8. HUNTSMAN SUIT TAILORED IN THE STEEL VIBE WITH PENNY COLLAR SHIRT BY BUDD

This company is also proud to carry out all its work in the UK, from initial concepts through to the completion of made-to-order and ready-to-wear garments, accessories and hand weaving. The catalogue includes an impressive and eclectic array of pieces: the Classic Jacket, Cycle Jacket, Scooter Coat, Wool Cap, Hat Scarf and even the Dashing Tweed Converse trainers that cut a real dash.

That's not to say Dashing Tweeds is entirely product-based. A number of international designers use the company's unique woven textiles to supplement their own designs. The textiles used are originally designed in the DT studio in London, woven in some of the most exclusive textile mills in Britain, before landing on exclusive store shelves around the world. Suffice it so say that the most exciting address of all must surely be, the inimitable Savile Row.

5

6

7

8

CHAPTER THREE

Accessories

A MINI-REVOLUTION IN
MEN'S JEWELLERY

Men and jewellery – two words which don't always sit happily together and which, from experience, flirt dangerously on the limits of tastelessness; think chest medallions and dodgy ID bracelets and most people shudder. Men are considered better-versed when it comes to buying women jewellery and yet Links of London has been creating something of a mini-revolution in men's jewellery for the past 20 years.

The story began when a restaurant owner requested fish cufflinks for their most loyal clients. As luck would have it, luxury store Harvey Nichols happened across them and fell in love with the fish, subsequently ordering the entire collection. This was a turning point for the company that brought heightened visibility beyond its wildest dreams.

Since then, Links of London has regularly created eclectic collections of silver and gold jewellery for men and women alike, and for three consecutive years has been named Jewellery Brand of the Year.

← 1. SALMON CUFFLINKS → 2. LONDON LANDMARK CUFFLINKS INSPIRED BY THE TWISTING ARCHITECTURE OF THE GHERKIN 3. THE SPORTY CHICANE WATCH

The key to Links of London's success lies in the elegant but understated designs; robust and modern rings are suitably modest for the British man and his lifestyle while accessories, like the London Landmark cufflinks, tip a wink to classic British humour. For an extra special touch, any piece can be engraved; particular favourites are the initialed cufflinks.

However, it is the watch collection that steals the limelight with its clever but subtle marriage of finely drawn designs and cutting-edge technology. The men's Chicane Watch is a contemporary work of art finished in stainless steel with a red, blue and black waterproof face. Meanwhile, traditionalists can't get enough of pieces like the Noble Rose

Gold Automatic Watch finished with its soft brown leather strap and gold and white Roman-numeral face.

It's a rare feat, but Links of London have perfected the art of practical yet beautiful jewellery for men without even a whiff of bling. Any gentleman looking to add a little shine to their wardrobe should consider a trip to Links of London – it may just cause a mini-revolution.

MULBERRY

CLASSIC LEATHER WITH ENGLISH SENSIBILITY

Think of the English countryside and you picture fluffy sheep, black-and-white cows grazing the fields and sleepy villages lost in a timeless era. This idyll in the heart of rural Somerset is the setting for Mulberry, a company whose history of luxury leather craftsmanship has been largely inspired by its natural surroundings.

Founded in 1971, Mulberry's roots are firmly entrenched in age-old saddlery techniques using the highest quality leather. The 1970s and '80s saw Mulberry embark on the production of quilted fishing and poacher bags, and classic outerwear. Never before had hard-wearing country attire looked this good and Mulberry soon became known for its own brand of "Style Anglais" long since being considered one of the first luxury lifestyle brands.

Today, the company's Somerset base at The Rookery has become the epicentre of bag production and one

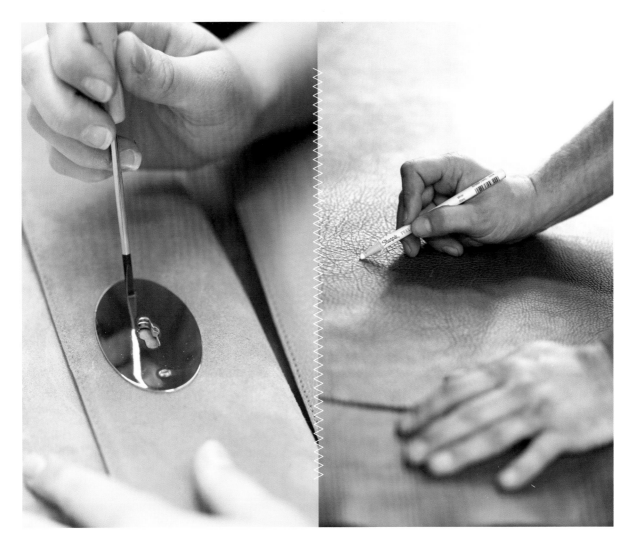

← 1. TONY IN CHOCOLATE → 2, 3. HANDMADE CRAFTSMANSHIP AT THE ROOKERY

of the last British luxury factories. Skills are strongly nurtured through Mulberry's exacting apprenticeship programme for future generations of craftspeople to be trained in collaboration with a local college. Alongside this and the creative family tree, there is a dynamic team of craftsmen and women all producing hundreds of bags a week. The opening of a second factory, close by in Bridgwater, in the summer of 2013, is set to double UK production.

The men's collections include classic bag designs, like the Elkington briefcase loved for its relaxed shape and soft leather, which ages particularly well in natural oak.

The discreet Tony features no external branding and is padded inside for laptop protection, twinning rich English craft with modern business attire. There are also some ingenious, elegant leather accessories, including the Mulberry iPad Folio in smooth Nappa leather and which comes in three sizes, and a variety of practical iPad sleeves, iPhone and Kindle covers, all embossed with the Mulberry tree logo – a sign of exceptional British leather craft heritage.

← 4. ELKINGTON IN OAK

→ 5. MULBERRY ADJUSTABLE IPAD SLEEVE IN BLACK

ETTINGER

ETTINGER...THE GROWING IMPORTANCE OF HAND-MADE IN BRITAIN

Setting foot in an Ettinger store provokes the same kind of wonder I imagine Roald Dahl's Charlie must have felt when he first set eyes on Willy Wonka's chocolate factory. Welcome to the Mecca of leather goods and accessories.

As you take in the beguiling scent of expensive leather and the hushed tones of an enraptured clientele, the sensory experience begins. There are rows upon rows of technicolour wallets of every conceivable shape, size and style: card holders, cash clips and coin cases, visiting card cases and zip wallets to name but a few. Take your pick from the myriad of collections on offer, though you may need a couple of hours; the selection is awe-inspiring. Variations on a theme mean you can plump for the softest of suedes or the sturdiest of leathers to befit your briefcase, suitcase or sports bag. There are hip flasks in duck-egg blue, double-bound photo frames in sleek black, BlackBerry Playbook clutch folders in sumptuous red and slate, silver cufflinks encased in regal purple leather inlay. Not before long, you start to question how you ever

← 1. WALLET DETAILS OF THE STRIKING "STERLING COLLECTION", SHOWN HERE IN PURPLE AND ORANGE → 2. THE HAND-GLUING PROCESS WHEN MAKING AN ETTINGER VISITING CARD CASE 3. HAND-MADE BRIDLE HIDE BILLFOLD WALLETS LINED UP AND AWAITING FINISHING TOUCHES IN THE ETTINGER FACTORY

lived without that natty tan-coloured magnifying glass not to mention its matching Maglite hand torch that you always wish you had when you're scrambling for the keys at the bottom of your bag.

There is something quite simply exquisite for every type of man, in every shade and in every grade of top-quality leather under the sun. Though the pleasure derived from these luxurious goods is most definitely sensorial, it most definitely isn't limited to that.

Ettinger's great pride and renown is thanks to the craftsmen and women behind the scenes. They are among the last to still make leather goods in the UK, but not without at least five years of full Ettinger training beforehand. A visit to the Ettinger factory would put paid to any doubts about the future of the leather goods industry. It's a hive of concentrated activity where every skill has its use and every craftsperson can fulfil a dream: pattern makers, sample makers, hand cutters, assemblers, stitchers and quality controllers. Everyone is vital, of course, and most learnt the art of leather-making during

← 4. ETTINGER'S LUXURY SHOWROOM AT ITS LONDON HEAD OFFICES IN PUTNEY
SW15 → 5. HAND TRIMMING AN ETTINGER BRIDGE HIDE COAT WALLET WITH
THE POPULAR LONDON TAN COLOUR INSIDE 6. ETTINGER'S BLACKBERRY
PLAYBOOK CLUTCH, COMMISSIONED BY BLACKBERRY 7. OX-BLOOD RED AND
ACORN COLOURED CLUTCHES MADE BY ETTINGER WITH LEADING BRITISH
TATTOO ARTIST, SAIRA HUNJAN'S STUNNING PHEASANT AND FOX HEAD
DESIGNS EMBOSSED ON THE OUTSIDE

their formative years. The leather is the star material here and
is sourced from a number of tanneries in the UK and abroad.
It arrives at Ettinger in whole skins that range from six to
60-square-feet in size, after which it is cut and the team perform
their magic before finishing and packing every piece by hand.

It is this attention to detail and faultless dexterity that Gerry
Ettinger so prized when he set about creating this business in
the 1950s. Ettinger was an accomplished businessman and
linguist whose travels and encounters fuelled an entrepreneurial
spirit and a keen eye for luxury. He acquired a small leather
goods manufacturing business, which had been making
leather goods in London since the 19th century, and used
this foundation of craftsmanship and design to build the
extraordinary business which Ettinger has become today.

Seek advice on their bespoke service for a special personalised
gift or even better: treat yourself to a monogrammed travel bag.

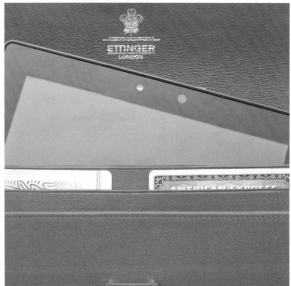

ASPINAL OF LONDON

FLAWLESS CRAFTSMANSHIP & STYLE, EXCLUSIVE DESIGN AND LUXURY LIFESTYLE

Handmade craftsmanship and excellence in design
are fundamental to Aspinal of London. The company
founded in 2002, has become synonymous with producing
quintessentially British high-quality leather goods. So coveted
are Aspinal's wares that clients will wait months to experience
the pleasure of owning them.

It would seem that success was written in the stars
for Aspinal. The driving force behind the company, Iain
Burton was a respected entrepreneur who brought with
him considerable creative experience. His career had to date
included some pioneering breakthroughs in music and sound,
notably as the largest provider of audio technology and
content in museums and galleries around the world. From this
erudite environment grew the seeds of a renaissance in the
dying British leather goods industry – Aspinal.

More than a decade later and you can browse through
luscious leathers and soft suedes, vegetable tanned and dyed

with natural plant extracts, and crafted by hand in the UK and Italy. There's charm in every piece, cared for with oils and beeswax that lend a signature aromatic scent to all things Aspinal.

Amazon crocodile calf brings texture and consistent finish to wallets and diaries, while lizard leather is popular for men's briefcases, bags and belts with its supple touch. Iain Burton wanted the quality of his products to be omnipresent: "… from the zips, to the silk linings hidden in every pocket".

Needless to say that Aspinal's bespoke service – your loved one's initials engraved inside a diary or a favourite clasp perhaps – makes it all the more gorgeous.

CUFFLINKS, SOPHISTICATED BAUBLES IN THE UNIVERSE OF MEN'S FASHION

piastra in corallo rosso
occhini in onyx
samepi in corallo bruno rosso

. piastra niodelinto fino

It was in 1876 that the eminent and rather aptly named goldsmith Benvenuto Villa (translated as "welcome home") established the first jewellery workshop in the heart of Milan. He was also an accomplished sculptor and alchemist whose prolific works had earned him numerous prestigious medals and awards, by the end of the 19th century, at the Exposition Universelle de Paris. Benvenuto was graced with talent, but also an immense personality. Eccentric and imaginative, he was renowned for being avant-garde in his work, introducing new and unknown precious alloys, such as black gold, into his creations.

He had a son, Giuseppe, who took the business to even greater heights. He was equally gifted and made a name creating sumptuous materials woven from gold thread.

Milanese society had long been renowned for an innate sense of dramatic style and showmanship. In no time, the Villa name had garnered more than a few loyal clients in the

← 1. PENDING JEWELLERY IN CORAL, WOOD, BARK, ONYX AND YELLOW GOLD 1930 → 2. HUMIDOR PENDANT IN ROCK CRYSTAL, ENAMEL, DIAMONDS WITH ROSE GOLD MOUNTS AND WHITE GOLD BAIL 3. FRUIT JELLY PENDANT IN BRONZE, HEMATITE AND WHITE GOLD BAIL

city, all of them eager to show off their spoils to an envious public gallery.

Success paved the way for further expansion and, by 1930, Villa's via Manzoni boutique had opened for business. This was an excellent opportunity, right after the First World War, for the company to carve a new niche, creating and refining precious stones for the glamour-starved elite and the Italian Royal Family. Burmese rubies, Kashmir sapphires, tremblant diamond necklaces and the Paesaggi or "Pastoral" brooches

bedecked in coloured stones – all were exquisite. Giuseppe must have felt proud as he witnessed Milan's high society turn out for the opening of the Teatro alla Scala draped in his decorative creations.

The fourth generation, Filippo and Marco, took over in 1980 and remain to this day. They take their craft very seriously and have studied extensively to point the company in new directions, especially for men's accessories. Alongside studies at the Gemmological Institute of America in New York, they

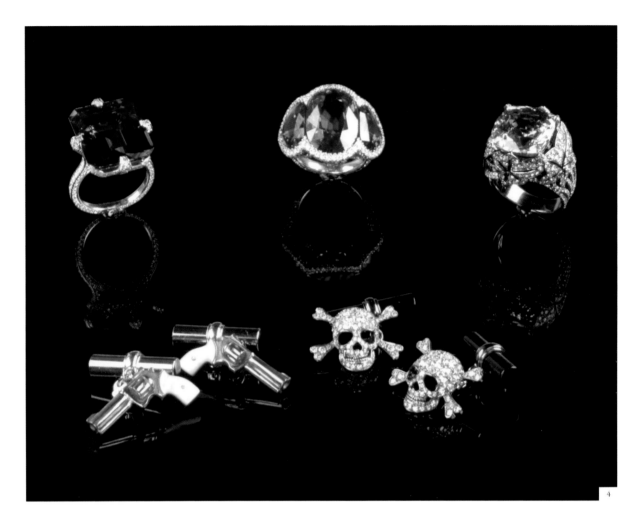

← 4. "CAGE" RING WITH EMERALD CUT TANZANITE CT. 25,02 AND DIAMONDS CT. 1,63 MOUNTED IN WHITE GOLD 18 KT / RING WITH 3 ORANGE GARNET CT. 27,30 AND DIAMONDS CT. 1,68 MOUNTED IN WHITE GOLD 18 KT / "IVY" RING WITH 1 CUSHON SHAPE MINT GROSSULAR CT. 13,84 AND ANTIQUE CUT DIAMONDS CT. 2,07 MOUNTED IN WHITE GOLD 18 KT / "GUNS" CUFFLINKS IN HEMATITE WITH ROUND BARS IN HEMATITE AND WHITE GOLD 18 KT / "SKULL" MICROMOSAIC CUFFLINKS IN DIAMONDS WITH ROUND BARS IN BLACK ONYX AND WHITE GOLD 18 KT → 5. 6. 7. CRAFTSMAN IN VILLA'S WORKSHOP 8. "ROSE" BROOCH WITH DIAMONDS CT. 18,78 AND WHITE GOLD 18 KT

have picked up some priceless nuggets of information from experienced stone traders around the world. They've injected modern themes into vintage or ancient styles, particularly with their striking Byzantine mosaic pieces. No room for the dull or ordinary here – Benvenuto would have approved.

Recent collections have included 15 different colours and tones of diamonds, rubies, emeralds, tanzanite, spinels, and peridots – blue, pink and yellow sapphires. Some of the most memorable pieces are the extraordinary cufflinks that have become a prized part of the Villa collection. We're treated to a symphony of jade, lapis lazuli, hematite, rare shells and "one-of-a-kind" pieces. Angels and demons, dog's heads, sparkling solitaires for the strong-minded, delicate buttons, material threaded knots, customised initials for the more discreet – all carefully crafted within Villa's Milan laboratory.

It was once said that "cufflinks are among the few types of men's jewellery considered to be socially credible, like watches and belt buckles: they are functional, thus acceptable". If you're going to start anywhere, start here.

5

6

7

8

PASSAGGIO CRAVATTE

STYLE, DISCRETION AND EXQUISITE BESPOKE TAILORING FROM ITALY'S LEADING TIE-MAKER

A well-dressed gentleman will live by the cut of his suit and the finishing details, an immaculate pair of shoes and an original tie. If he can't get to the tailor, then the tailor will come to him, no matter where he may be in the world. This is where *Passaggio Cravatte* steps in, with stunning personalised ties. Infinite possibilities – colour, cloth, pattern, shape and size – bring the crucial finishing touch, with an almighty flourish in the case of *Passaggio Cravatte*.

A label born from a long-lived desire to think outside the "ready-made" box, Passaggio Cravatte was founded by two young entrepreneurs, Gianni Cerutti and his wife Marta Passaggio. They took it upon themselves to carve a market for the one-of-a-kind tie experience; one that allowed the customer to select design and materials for their own tie. The goal was to create an exclusive product, true to Neapolitan tradition and close to their hearts.

The selection at Passaggio Cravatte is impressive, with the finest vintage silks, wools, and thousands of authentic and

← 1. THE DETAIL OF THE HEM IS MADE BY HAND ON PRECIOUS JACQUARD
FABRIC. → 2. AN ELEGANT CRAVAT FROM THE WOODEN DISPLAY; A SAMPLE
FROM THE TIE. 3. FOUR HANDS WORKING ON PROFESSIONAL TOOLS WITH
PRECIOUS SILK.

mixed fabrics, many from the 1940s and 1950s as well as
jacquard and regimental patterns from the 1930s. The dull
and ordinary have been banished – think beautiful, brightly
coloured stripes, paisley and floral patterns, all hand-stamped
and therefore utterly unique. Customers attest to the selection
experience being as valuable as the tie itself. Personality is
the key to the end-result, while Gianni and Marta's approach
is personable, intuitive and engaging. As the only employees
that customers come into contact with (only one seamstress
cuts each tie to guarantee perfect continuity), they treat each
gentleman like family, for whom each carefully posed stitch
matters as much as the last. Fittings and discussions can be
arranged anywhere in Italy, on-site in Passaggio's Milan and

Naples quarters or, if necessary and within reason, through
technological communication.

Choosing the fabric, model, lining and the number of folds you
prefer is a refreshingly enjoyable and imaginative process, not
least because of Gianni's involvement. He has always strongly
maintained that the knot is the tie's most personal feature. For
example, the luxurious old-style seven-ply is an exceptional
model made from one piece of silk and it is considered by most to
be the Rolls-Royce of neckties. For extra interest, you can even
have your initials or family crest embroidered on the finished
piece in a variety of wonderfully woven threads. The selection is
the most time-consuming part of the experience so allow plenty

← 4. CLASSIC TIE WITH VINTAGE SILK → 5. THE SILK IS SPREAD OUT WITH THE PAPER TEMPLATE TO THE BESPOKE MEASUREMENTS 6. THE SILK IS CUT ENTIRELY BY HAND ACCORDING TO THE CLIENTS MEASUREMENTS 7. CHECKING THE CUT SILK IS TO THE CORRECT MEASUREMENTS 8. THE INTERNAL LINING IS INSERTED, THE WEIGHT OF WHICH IS CHOSEN TO THE CLIENTS NEEDS 9. THE TIE IS STAPLED BY HAND USING SMALL PINS BEFORE BEING READY TO BE STITCHED 10. THE TIE IS STITCHED BY HAND FOLLOWING A TECHNIQUE OVER 100 YEARS OLD

of time for this as it is not only fundamental, but also Gianni and Marta's way of making you get the best out of your tie. Once designed, the actual creation of a tie can be swift, taking anything from 40 minutes to four hours. The attention to detail in the final piece would suggest four months, however.

With such an infectious passion for their craft and a great respect for their customers, how could any Passaggio Cravatte gentleman not feel that little bit more special than the rest?

5

6

7

8

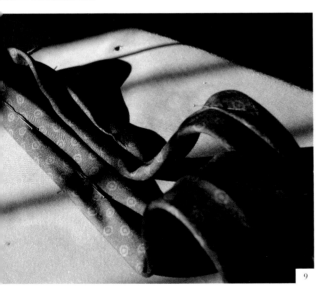

9

10

RICCARDO BESTETTI

THE BEST ITALIAN BESPOKE SHOES

As part of Italy's growing stable of bespoke craftsmen, Riccardo Freccia Bestetti's single-minded approach has paid off. The Milanese artisan's shoe creations are never short of exquisite, but they're also daring. They celebrate elegance with a generous dash of eccentricity – much like Riccardo himself. Every stage of his creation process is carried out by hand in the tiny Vigevano laboratory he likes to call his "headquarters". He prefers to be tucked away here, far from any "ill advisers for whom machines are sadly of paramount importance".

In 1994, Maestro Bestetti was on a trip to Texas when he purchased a pair of traditional made-to-measure Texan boots. Although they'd been tailored to the specific shape of his feet, Riccardo was not entirely satisfied and visited Texas on several occasions to glean what he could from the older Texan bootmakers. He learnt to "steal with the eyes", effectively observing trade secrets and returned to Italy with one single

← 1. THREE SHOES ENTIRELY HAND-MADE JUST AFTER THE HOLE-MAKING → 2. CROCODILE UPPERS ARE HAND-STITCHED AT ALL THE VARIOUS PRODUCTION STAGES · 3. BESIDE, HAND-MEASUREMENT SHOE LAST AND WOODEN SOLE ENTIRELY HAND

objective: to create and manufacture made-to-order, handmade Texan cowboy boots.

Thanks to his extraordinary talent, Riccardo cultivated a client base right across the globe, revelling in the different styles and ideas he encounters. Some of his clients' more lavish tastes have pushed Riccardo to stretch himself, but he would say they merely drive him to perfection. Riccardo is proud that his shoes are made-to-measure, and that they adhere perfectly to the shape and movement of the foot. He has succeeded where others might not – producing eclectic and exclusive Texan cowboy boots that have lost none of their original character.

CHEANEY SHOES

MADE IN ENGLAND
WORN AROUND
THE WORLD

You can tell a lot about a man from his shoes. For some they are purely functional, while for others they not only complete an outfit, they define the wearer. One thing is certain: it is your shoes that will determine the way you carry yourself – and therefore, to a great extent, how you feel – on any particular day.

So where to start? The choice can be overwhelming. What you must look for, no matter what, is enduring quality. For a discerning businessman and gentleman, quality should rank above everything, including fashion.

One company that has delivered unwavering and flawless quality is Cheaney, thanks to more than 125 years of traditional methods and meticulous craftsmanship.

The Cheaney story began in Northamptonshire; the region had been the pulsing heart of the shoe industry since the 17th century. Yet there had been few or no shoe factories involved

← 1. HOT UPPERS ARE HUMIDIFIED FOR A MINIMUM OF 48 HOURS TO SOFTEN THE LEATHER → 2. TWEED BOOTS AWAITING THEIR QUALITY CONTROL INSPECTION 3. LEATHER IS CUT BY HAND BY SKILLED CLICKERS

in the entire shoe-making process previously (every stage was carried out in separate premises sometimes miles apart).

It was Joseph Cheaney who set a precedent when in 1886 he established J. Cheaney, Boot & Shoemakers on a small site in Desborough before moving to new premises ten years later (which they still occupy today). They made their name during one of the busiest and most fraught periods of the 20th century, the First World War. With exceptional skill, the company was producing a staggering 2,500 pairs of shoes a week, all hand-stitched and screwed. The future was set. The company moved with the times and the quality remains as Cheaney now stands as one of the few remaining family-owned British shoemakers to craft all its products entirely in England, from the first stitch to the final polish.

Full-grain calf leather, sourced from around Europe, is chosen for its soft, comfortable and breathable character. Colours and finish are selected to complement a specific style and design, not the other way around.

The shoe-lining is complete and made from leather, rather than partial or made from textile. A leather-lined shoe can absorb moisture from the foot throughout the day and release it after wear, and so it's true to say that a Cheaney shoe will fit like a glove and feel like a slipper.

4

← 4. UPPER STITCHING IN THE CLOSING ROOM → 5. 'IRVINE' BOOTS WITH SHEARLING LINING 6. DECORATIVE MARKINGS ARE MADE TO THE SHOE SOLE AND EDGE
7. HAND PUNCHING A TONGUE 8. CHEANEY SOLE STAMP MARK IS APPLIED TO EVERY PAIR

So what keeps the shoe intact? The heel and the sole are crucial and Cheaney shoes are miles ahead of their game. Leather heels are terrifically sturdy, while leather soles are stitched, rather than glued or nailed, to the upper-shoe. This is the Goodyear welted process which makes these extraordinary shoes more robust and supportive than usual. It also means you can replace a pair's soles several times through Cheaney's refurbishment service, without ever affecting the integrity of the construction.

A pair of Cheaney shoes will take eight weeks to make using 160 processes. There are plenty of beautiful original or classic styles to suit a country pursuit, a formal dinner or a business meeting. The icing on the cake is the more you wear your Cheaney shoes, the more comfortable they become as the leather adapts to the shape of the foot. Intelligence and natural beauty rolled into one. What gentleman could resist?

5

6

7

8

JIMMY CHOO

CONFIDENT, OVERTLY MASCULINE STYLE WITH A REFINED SENSE OF DETAIL

Jimmy Choo launched their Men's Collection in 2011 and it has quickly established a reputation for fusing modern British style with luxurious Italian craftsmanship and innovative use of materials.

The collection strikes a perfect balance between classicism and rock'n'roll style, effortlessly dressing the Jimmy Choo men for going out, going to work, working it or just hanging out.

For autumn-winter, the collection is a focused but versatile lifestyle offering, covering several moods ranging from more formal styles, such as lace-ups, monk straps, loafers, side-zip boots and slippers, and rugged masculine boots, such as Chelsea boots and Bikers. Trainers appear detailed in both subtle and more eccentric materials.

The main inspiration for the Men's Collection was a moment in time, early-'80s New York and evenings spent at

← 1. SLOANE IN BLACK GLITTER.   → 2. DARBY IN BLACK SHINY CALF AND SATIN 3. > RIFORD IN BLACK CALF LEATHER

Mr Chow's with artistic luminaires such as Basquiat, Warhol and Clemente. New wave, influenced by punk and glam rock, up-ended traditional conventions of men's fashion. Sandra Choi, creative director, comments: "We were channelling an early-'80s dandyism with influences ranging from preppy, to military, to street style."

There's a playful element to the creations that takes the codes of classic men's style and infuses them with a modern sensibility. The signature style "Sloane" loafer is a contemporary interpretation of the gentleman's evening slipper, in black coarse glitter, while the Darblay is a more traditional penny loafer, routed in the '50s with an ironic twist – the silhouette of a burlesque woman engraved on the penny.

To mark the launch of the Dover Street store in spring 2013, the scorpion adorns the Sloane slipper in statement gold brocade, evolving into a brand signature as a subtle silver-embossed talisman on the sole of all shoes.

SHOES YOU CAN ATTACH SOME ROMANCE TO

"Educating the man who only wears sneakers" is a phrase coined by Mr Hare. Marc Hare, a dreadlocked surfer from Croydon, is a refreshingly original creator whose eponymous brand is responsible for some of the most versatile shoes in Mayfair. With decades of experience in marketing, Marc reached a critical point in 2008 when his fortunes were against him. He lost his job, went through a divorce and dislocated his knee – an injury that annoyingly prevented him from surfing. It was at this moment that Marc embarked on a "tapas road trip" in the foothills of Spain's Sierra Nevada mountains.

The concept of Mr Hare was as unplanned as his original trip. The seeds of change were sown one fine day in a tapas bar as Marc sat admiring the woven sandals of an elderly drinker. Marc could see there was room for improvement in these sandals with a few small tweaks. So he set about tweaking.

Five years on and Mr Hare has the luxury of designing his shoes wherever he so chooses. Currently it's Empoli in Tuscany.

← 1 . . . . → 2 . . . . 3 . . . .

He calls Mr Hare a "black shoe brand" because the designs are perfect for stylish evening wear. There's a shoe for every setting of course, from a bar in Soho to a beach shack on the Bermuda shores. Marc is eager to stress that he isn't limited to evening wear, though he loves the thought of his friends dancing the night away in a pair of Mr Hare's shoes.

JUST BLAZE

BEYOND PATIENCE
LIES THE SKY

French luxury lifestyle entrepreneur and fashion designer, Kadir Oketokoun, founded Just Blaze, also known as DVO Bello, in 2007. Kadir's first innovative design with Just Blaze took five intense years of research and development in the making – the first authentic cashmere T-shirt. His mission was to create a bespoke T-shirt from an unusual material, in this case the purest and thinnest form of cashmere, which would allow for easy summer wear. The noble material is sourced in Nepal where local craftsmen make the T-shirt by hand.

The inspiration for Just Blaze's logo motif was the beauty of simple lines, allowing the cashmere garment to speak for itself. There are currently five different designs of T-shirt that clients can select as their bespoke template – two short-sleeved (round and V-neck), two long-sleeved (round and V-neck) and the long-sleeved turtleneck.

This collection of cashmere creations features a range of limited-edition colours. For added interest, new colours will be

← 1. ON MAIN MANIFOLD 21 → 2. ON THE SWING, DOWN THE BACK AND ON THE 3. IN THE REGION CASE

introduced with the advent of every new cashmere collection.
Look out for black and gold in the first collection that looks
destined to make a dazzling impression. Kadir Oketokoun is
constantly searching and pushing for new ideas to work with in
cashmere. His wealth of knowledge on this rare and luxurious
material promises some very exciting projects ahead.

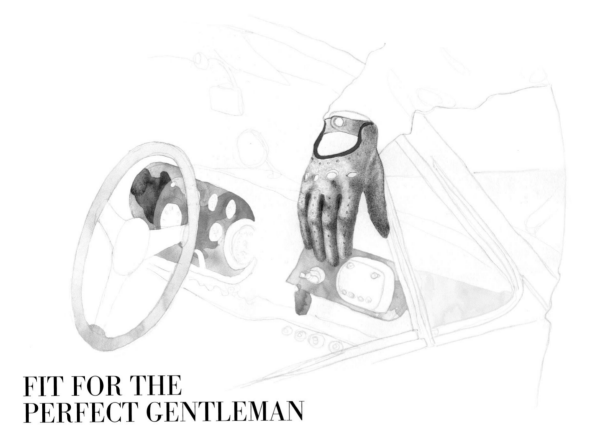

FIT FOR THE
PERFECT GENTLEMAN

Some say your hands are one of most important features a person will notice about you. Think of the handshake or the wave. A single movement can betray as much grace as a carefully constructed ensemble and impeccable grooming.

Dents established in 1777, is a company that knows all about expert glove making and, though the company is based in Warminster in rural south-west England, its reputation is global. People travel far and wide to get hold of their Dents gloves: most notably a Japanese businessman with connecting flights at Heathrow, who managed to factor in a quick trip to Warminster, where he collected hoards of gifts from the Dents head office, before dashing back to Heathrow to catch his connecting flight home.

Stories like these aren't unusual, however, given the exceptionally beautiful items that emerge from Dents workshops and the personal service. Heritage and tradition

← 1. DENTS SOFTEST WHITE KID GLOVE IN TONAL COLOURS WITH LINEN CORDS
→ 2. 1777 HERITAGE RANGE, STITCHED WITH THE DENTS FLORAL PERFORATION IN WILTSHIRE 3. TWO-HAND TAILORED RED DEERSKIN TRADITIONAL DENTS STITCHED ON FOUR-BUTTON THUMB LOCK STYLE

are the backbone of this business, and there are traces of historical craftsmanship in everyday use. It's not uncommon for old working Singer sewing machines to be used and kept for future replacement parts. Dents even make individually bench-cut gloves, made from the highest quality peccary skins, one of the rarest leathers available. The Heritage Collection includes seldom-used leathers for its luxurious items, such as North American deerskin and fine aniline Ethiopian hair sheep.

Every detail is painstakingly applied. Look closely and you'll see tiny distinctive shaped cuts of leather at the base of the finger that achieve that "fits like a glove" feeling.

SHARP & DAPPER

SHARP&DAPPER

A MINOR
LIFE-CHANGING
EXPERIENCE

Looking ultra-sharp can call for a lot of "behind the scenes" upholstery. Any man chained to his desk at work or who spends a lot of time getting up and down all day knows that the "constant tucking in of the shirt" syndrome is more than a little annoying. Shirt stays – a sort of upside-down braces invention – were reinvented in 2011, but look set to revolutionise the future of shirt-wearing. It's a simple system, but incredibly effective, not to mention aesthetically pleasing. The slim braces anchor the shirt safely within the trouser waist, acting as the holding force between the socks and the shirt tails. As a result, your shirt remains safely tucked in all day – quite wonderfully so as well. In fact, they're so comfortable that Johan Ekelund, the director and co-creator of Sharp & Dapper, swears by them and wears a pair every day to work, even when he comes in on his natty Sharp & Dapper branded scooter.

The Sharp & Dapper shirt stays are part of a greater catalogue of ingenious and slick men's accessories that

← 1. [...] → 2. [...] 3. [...]

include old favourites like braces, clip-on buttons and socks. The braces (or suspenders as some know them) are classically elegant. Traditionally, braces were buttoned to the waistline, effectively strapping the wearer in. Sharp & Dapper has overcome this problem with clip-on buttons for extra versatility and a streamlined silhouette. All the company's wares are produced in London's Notting Hill, but are available exclusively online at sharpanddapper.com

OLIVER PEOPLES CELEBRATES 25 YEARS OF LA STYLE

How you view the world is your choice, but it's fair to say that things look decidedly rosier on a bright sunny day, through a good pair of sunglasses. Oliver Peoples knows all about sunny days. Founded in California, this company tells of a life we all aspire to, in which surfing, swimming and afternoons by the sea are par for the course. LA style. Larry Leight envisioned all of these in his youth; as a keen surfer and traveller, he sought a career that would allow for freedom and creativity. After qualifying as an optician, he founded Oliver Peoples and launched the first original collection in 1987. The venture was a success right from the start.

The company has launched a number of special categories (from steel-rimmed and vintage aviator sunglasses, to classic horn-rimmed) and been involved in some impressive developments over the years. There have also been some thought-provoking short films, notably for the company's 25th anniversary in 2013. Staying true to the brand's LA roots, the celebratory campaign

← 1. [illegible] → 2. [illegible]

3. [illegible] 4. [illegible]

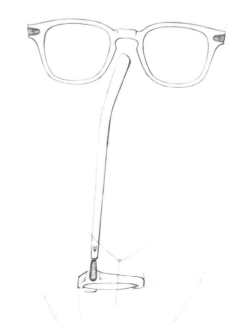

featured Ray Liotta and Bar Paly, and was directed by
Patrick Hoelck, who stylishly brought to life the limited
edition anniversary collection. Filmed on Stage 9 of the
Sony Studios lot in Culver City, California, the campaign
represented the spirit of an iconic brand and was inspired
from Larry Leight's 1989 archive sketches.

CHAPTER FOUR

Pursuit

RAY WARD

THE BEST THINGS
COME IN PAIRS...

In the world of hunting, there are some hard-and-fast rules to observe. On the field, it is knowledge, a keen eye for detail and gut instinct that are your greatest allies. Behind the scenes, your gunsmith is your mentor. In a specialised trade such as this, only the rare few stand the test of time: hunters are exacting and the market is tough.

Those seeking advice on the sport of hunting take comfort in the years of experience and the wisdom a gunsmith can impart. Ray Ward is such a company, with an enviable reputation for delivering the most exquisite shotguns and rifles from world-renowned brands, such as James Purdey and Sons, Boss & Co and Watson Bros. On celebrating their 50th anniversary, the company made the leap to become gun makers in their own right and now stock stunning pieces from their eponymous range at their flagship Knightsbridge premises.

The business dates back to 1961 and a gun store in Surrey. What started as a simple, albeit expert, supplier of sporting

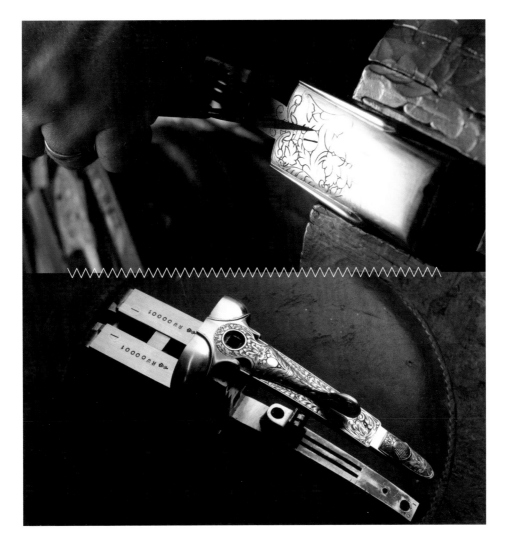

← 1. THE FIRST PAIR OF RAY WARD GUNS TO BE COMPLETED → 2. THE MARKS AND ABBREVIATIONS TRACE EVERY PROCESS IN PRODUCING THE GUNS ENGRAVED ALONG THE 3. THE FINISHED ACTION OF THE VERY FIRST RAY WARD GUN

goods has since changed locations, and evolved into a comprehensive service that supplies the highest quality specialist hunting and shooting equipment from the UK and around the world. The clientele is loyal and discerning with a taste for luxury, and customer guidance must therefore be insightful and honest, whether it be on gun servicing and reparation or care and gun storage.

Ray Ward's passion propelled him to national and European titles in numerous clay shooting disciplines. He was chairman and then president of the Clay Pigeon Shooting Association in the UK, where he remains the life vice-president.

His legacy lives on through his son and grandson, both of whom have made their mark and earned respect within the industry. His youngest son John is heavily involved in the Ray Ward business and keeps the flame burning. The setting, in the heart of London's most illustrious neighbourhood, would suggest that it has never burned more brightly.

TRADITIONAL BRITISH GUN MAKERS WITH MORE THAN 150 YEARS OF SPORTING HERITAGE

The tradition of shooting has played an integral part in British country life for centuries. Be it grouse on the Yorkshire Moors or pheasants in Devon, the English countryside has served as the field for this royal sport since prehistoric times. Fast forward to present day and the prestigious company Holland & Holland, which has transformed the sport into an iconic art form since it was founded in the mid-19th century.

The founder, Harris Holland began manufacturing rifles in 1850. He took on his nephew, Henry Holland, as his apprentice and thus the company became Holland & Holland. The duo worked together to perfect the art of gun making. Nearly two centuries after Harris Holland's first steps, the company continues to thrive on a truly global scale with locations in London, New York and Moscow. Holland & Holland's craftsmen still ply their trade at the London factory today.

← 1. BRITISH MANUFACTURING AND CRAFTSMANSHIP ARE KEY TO CREATING HOLLAND & HOLLAND'S COLLECTION OF SHOOTING CLOTHING AND ACCESSORIES. → 2. DUE TO THE PRECISE ATTENTION TO DETAIL AND HAND CRAFTSMANSHIP, IT CAN TAKE UP TO 1200 MAN-HOURS TO MAKE ONE OF HOLLAND & HOLLAND'S FAMOUS ROYAL SHOTGUNS. 3. HOLLAND & HOLLAND, THE FINEST BRITISH LONDON GUNROOM IS LOCATED ON BRUTON STREET IN THE HEART OF MAYFAIR.

The company prides itself on offering bespoke gun fittings and lessons on their own shooting grounds just 17 miles from central London. Here, shots can enjoy the 60 acres of rolling woodland and open countryside to master their shooting.

Holland & Holland has a stunning clothing collection that includes a range of shooting tweeds, moleskin trousers, a luxurious range of silks, as well as a safari collection for those African adventures. So if you aspire to the British ideal of shooting with a beautiful, bespoke gun by your side, we think you will find what you're looking for with Holland & Holland.

THE DALMORE BESPOKE IS A MALT WHISKY EXPERIENCE LIKE NO OTHER

In 1263, an ancestor of Clan Mackenzie spared King Alexander III from being slain by a stag thanks to a timely single shot of his arrow. As a sign of gratitude, the king bequeathed him the right to bear a stag's head upon his coat of arms, from which point every bottle issued from Mackenzie's Dalmore Distillery has borne this noble emblem.

The company as it is today was founded by Alexander Matheson in 1839, and now stands as Whyte and Mackay's largest distillery and the brand's flagship. The ancient venue is indeed majestic, overlooking the rugged green farmlands of Scotland. Dalmore's oldest and rarest stocks of Highland malt can be found here, drawn from casks that have been maturing since 1964. Master distiller Richard Paterson takes clients through a tasting process in the build up to their tailor-made package that comes complete with crystal decanter. Known as the Dalmore Bespoke Experience, this process

produces some of the most remarkable bottles ever seen. There is also a limited edition model for which only three highly prized bottles have ever been made – the Dalmore 64 Trinitas, for example, is worth US$160,000.

With four pairs of stills, Dalmore has a capacity of 4.2 million litres per annum and operates at near capacity. Scottish law requires whisky to be matured in oak wood which lends the whisky exquisite flavour; American oak adds accents of vanilla and coconut, and English oak lends fresh red fruit tones.

Dalmore custodians can attend exclusive bottling and Dalmore events, while the Dalmore Bespoke Experience also delivers one-of-a-kind luxury stays that include a weekend at the private Carnegie Club, Skibo Castle, with transport via helicopter escort.

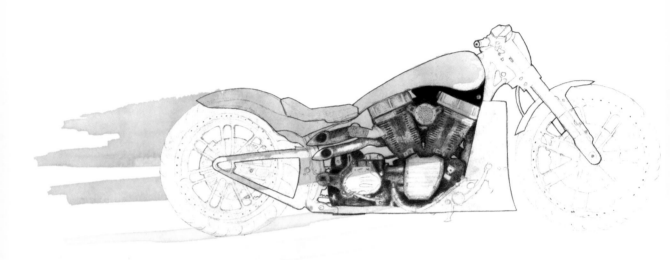

MORE THAN A
MOTORCYCLE...

Harley-Davidson is a brand name so strong that it has come, by virtue of association, to stand for long-haired bikers with a growl that means business and impossibly high handlebars.

Shaw Speed & Custom has successfully bucked the clichéd trend by customising the Harley-Davidson bike to suit any manner of rider nowadays. Here is a multi-award winning company based in the south of England, near Brighton, that has given the global industry a run for its money. Such a coup is well-deserved and, when you consider the customer service involved, it's no surprise that seasoned and novice riders are sitting up to take notice.

There's always room for some VIP treatment as well. As a Harley-Davidson dealer, the Speed Shop - as the service is also known - provides a Custom Suite. It's an exclusive area within the heart of the technical department, overlooking the workstations, where the nitty-gritty work takes place: full bike customisation. The best approach is for the client to

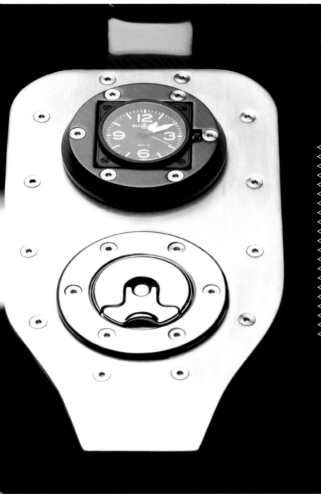

← 1. THE BELL & ROSS BR 01-92 CARBON FIBER DIAL INSPIRED BY A CAFÉ RACER, MEASURES 46MM × 46MM. LAUNCHED IN 2010 → 2. THE COCKPIT BELL & ROSS INSTRUMENTS PERFECTLY SUITED TO THE ANTIQUE STYLE OF THE CAFÉ RACER. 3. THE NASCAFÉ RACER BUILT ON A BIKE WHICH WAS CRAFTED BY THE SHAW MOTORCYCLE GARAGE OF THE UK. THE BIKE WON A VICTORY TITLE IN THE WORLD IN 2011.

schedule a consultation on site with an expert to record and assess all data gathered. No job is too small or too complex and the client can be involved every step of the way, be it a refurbishment job, some fresh paintwork or a complete Harley-Davidson overhaul. A custom bike will be entirely your own, and yes, that includes the fenders and gas tanks, right through to the handlebars and exhausts. A biker's dream, surely.

Unlike a lot of custom motorcycles that emerge from garages around Europe and the US, those being created and converted in the workstations at the Speed Shop can actually be ridden rather than merely admired. Keep your eyes peeled as the

Speed Shop is currently working on bikes from clients in Beirut, Dubai, Milan and Las Vegas, as well all over the UK.

Glamorous though it may seem, it's a tough and demanding industry, but that didn't stop Shaw Speed & Custom from fighting off some stiff competition in 2010, to win the annual Sturgis AMD World Championship of Bike Building. The Strike True II was the victory bike in question, no doubt making its private owner extremely proud. It seems quite fitting that the latter was inspired to name the great machine in memory of his grandfather's service in the RAF during the Second World War. The RAF Bombers Command and the bike's moniker, "Strike Hard, Strike Sure", couldn't have been

4

← 4. THE NASCAFE RACER SIDE ON, A BIKE WHICH WAS QUOTED BY THE
TOP MOTORCYCLE BLOGS AT BEING THE MOST FAMOUS MOTORCYCLE IN
THE WORLD IN 2011 → 5. THE REAR END OF THE XLST3 SPORTSTER A BIKE
EVENTUALLY GOING TO STOCKHOLM 6. THE ENGINE START BUTTON ON THE
XLST3, DETAIL COME NATURALLY TO THE SPEED SHOP 7. THE FRONT END OF
THE NASCAFE RACER

more apt. The design reflected a vintage feel, with a low-slung
appearance giving the curious impression that the bike was in
high-speed motion when actually standing still.

Aside from working with private individuals, Shaw Speed
& Custom also commissions for a number of corporate
partners. So what could a watchmaker and a motorcycle
have in common for example? Well, the complications of the
watchmaking process inspired the company to transform and
produce the Bell & Ross Nascafe Racer. As in watchmaking,
every single nut and bolt was stripped down and re-worked,
resulting in one of the most iconic machines to ever come out
of the Speed Shop Sussex workshop.

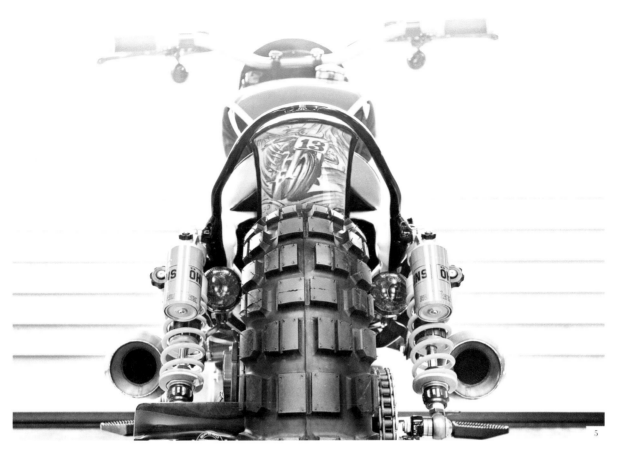

5

6

7

MURDOCK LONDON

LUXURY MALE GROOMING FROM LONDON'S PREMIER BARBERSHOPS

The word "barber" can have connotations for many of the traditional all-male shop, dense with the lingering smell of All Spice. Nowadays, Murdock London has achieved a thoroughly modern gentlemen-only salon that remains true to the barbershop experience and heritage. Four of these fabulous spaces are dotted around London and if you prefer your treatment to be unequivocally masculine, Murdock London has pulled it off.

The environment is relaxing and the services just varied enough to not be overwhelming: from the luxury wet-shave with conventional cutthroat razor, to haircuts, revitalising facials, shoe shining and essential grooming products. Visitors become "regulars" and build up a relationship with their barber – something of a lost tradition that was very important among the higher social classes in early-20th-century England.

The signature Murdock collection stocks some coveted fragrances and shaving tools that are all hand-made in Britain

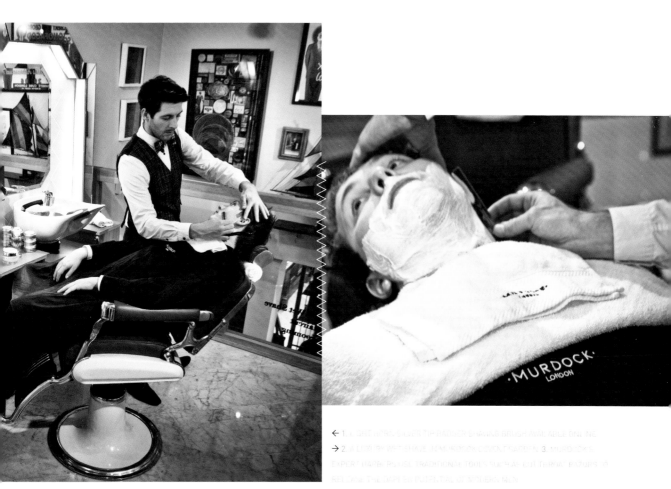

← 1. One pure silver-tip badger shaving brush available online
→ 2. A luxury wet-shave team Murdock cover four men 3. Murdock's expert barbers use traditional tools such as cut-throat razors to release the deeper potential of modern men

with the utmost attention to quality and workmanship. Skincare products are made by Murdock London in-house and entirely from natural ingredients to avoid chemical build-up on the skin. Every Murdock barber has extensive experience and a bank of knowledge to set you on your way to looking sharp and offers handy tips to keep your barber-fresh look for as long as possible – this, and a quick tipple of Three Wood whisky, are sure to add a spring to your step.

CHAPTER   FIVE

Articles

YOUR BESPOKE TOUR GUIDE

GIANNI CERUTTI

translated by Brian Grainger

Passaggio Cravatte has the noblest of intentions: to bring foreign customers and friends a taste of "bespoke" Italian brands, off the beaten track. For Passaggio Cravatte doesn't only produce handmade vintage fabric ties, it also offers discovery tours around venues of excellence. The company's luxury-savvy owners schedule customer appointments with the elite in Italian fashion. The service is personalised and geared to the specific needs of the client. Exclusivity and total discretion are guaranteed.

Gianni Cerutti of Passaggio Cravatte: "The client is asked to set out what he's looking or hoping for, in writing. Once we have that, we search through our extensive network of partner suppliers to identify the best match. Though the partners work in different fields, they all have the seal of excellence and are considered the very best craftsmen of bespoke products in Italy. Our selection criteria are very rigorous and exacting. We demand excellence of craftsmanship, design and aesthetic beauty in producing bespoke items to fit our client's specific requirements.

The client is introduced to the appropriate bespoke craftsman and Passagio Cravatte takes charge of the client's every need throughout his stay. We have established agreements with the best luxury hotels and first-class restaurants. We also ensure the client experiences the crème de la crème of Italian style across the arts, culture and history, and naturally the finest Italian food and wine – all against the backdrop of the country's beautiful landscape. It's a taste of 'la dolce vita' that we offer."

So what products are we talking about and who are these craftsmen?

GC: "We have access to an incredibly diverse range of products, including suits, shirts, shoes, cufflinks, sweaters, gloves, neckties, hats and spectacles, through to accessories such as pipes, coat hangers and bicycles. We could even introduce you to one of the world's finest sculptors who specialises in coats of arms.

"These 'specialised' artisans are deserving of their description – their creations are special, luxurious and unique, because bespoke really does mean 'the only one of its kind in the world'. Skilled experts will magic anything you choose to fit your requirements, from a pair of shoes to a set of cufflinks or suitcases, with a tie, hat and a silk handkerchief in between.

→ 1. BESPOKE CUFFLINKS BY DAVIDE SUTTON, ENTIRELY HANDCRAFTED IN WHITE GOLD
WITH COLOURED GEMS.

2

"A case in point is the Neapolitan tailor, Mimmo Pirozzi, who can still hand stitch a jacket in his workshop, using methods that date back to the 1800s and the Neapolitan School of Tailors.

"The results are astonishingly elegant. Maestro Mimmo firmly believes that the art of tailoring isn't only based on traditional hand stitching, but also on passion. Passion inspires his craft, flows through his work and can be seen in his every stitch.

"Another example is the d'Avino shirt maker in Naples where it takes some 32 man-hours to sew a single shirt as the artisans refuse to resort to the use of sewing machines. Maestro d'Avino, who also belongs to a long line of Neapolitan craftsmen, focuses on made-to-measure pieces, using a successful century-old process. The templating for shoulders and sleeves, for example, is as meticulous as for a made-to-measure suit.

"You'll also find tools of the trade that date back to the early-1900s at Il Vecchio Drappiere in Milan. Stepping into their workshop is like stepping back in time to Milan 50 years ago, when the fashion trade had yet to be industrialised; back in time, to the days when you would visit the drapers to buy your cloth and then find a tailor to fit you for a made-to-measure suit. Today, Il Vecchio Drappiere is still the 'go-to' address in Milan for those in the know, looking for the ultimate weave of cloth – cashmere, wool, solaro and the ultra-rare vicuña. Quality and durability are the buzzwords here.

"Davide Solazzi from Parma fashions bespoke cufflinks with diamond and other precious-stone inlays. He is one of the very few craftsmen left in this field. He uses no machinery, and so he and his wife create and cut cufflinks by hand at their workshop.

"Last but not least is Riccardo Bestetti from Vigevano, reputed to be among the finest shoemakers in the world. His shoes are renowned for their comfort, style and exceptional attention to detail. They will mold to the shape of the foot. Their elegance harks back to the Italy of the 1950s, the Roman 'dolce vita' era of fashion. Other shoe models draw on the 1800's, a time when dandies would be seen strolling through the streets in their finest shoes with walking stick, top hat and tails."

To sample our services, simply e-mail your request to us at info@passaggiocravatte.com Once Passaggio Cravatte has contacted you, you can start exploring the wonders of Italian savoir-faire. You'll discover tiny workshops and laboratories, made-to-measure and bespoke treasures that don't bow to the pressures of trends or mass appeal. We'll help you find your own style and elegance to reflect who you really are.

5

→ 5. MAESTRO MIMMO PIROZZI BRINGS THE THE FINAL TOUCHES TO AN UNLINED JACKET WITH ARRICCIO AND MARTINGALE ENTIRELY HANDMADE TO MEASURE.

THE AUTHENTIC GENTLEMAN'S WARDROBE

GIANNI CERUTTI

translated by Brian Grainger

Have you ever wondered what makes a gentleman's wardrobe and what its key pieces should be? The answer lies in Italy where I met Domenico Pirozzi, the man largely responsible for dressing, among others, the much-loved Italian screen legend, the elegant Totò. Domenico, or Mimmo to his friends, is the last in a line of traditionally schooled Neapolitan tailors. Remarkably, he started out as an apprentice in the trade at the tender age of eight. Domenico's creations are highly covetable. Possessed of enviable style and singular character, these garments are head-turners for all the right reasons. Domenico's hand-made creations are considered to be Neapolitan masterpieces.

Should a gentleman's wardrobe draw on the same pieces all year round?
Domenico Pirozzi: "Absolutely not. You'll be freezing in winter and boiling hot in summer. Fabrics used to serve throughout the year have no place in the world of Pirozzi tailoring."

So how do you choose your winter wear?
DP: "In winter, an elegant gent would own about four overcoats: 1 A blue cashmere double-breasted Chesterfield for the theatre and grand occasions 2 A six-button, double-breasted Polo jacket in camel-coloured leather, with a loose half-belt at the back, lapels and hand-stitched sleeves 3 Two three-button Crombie coats – one grey and one dark blue – the latter should be ultra-smart and single-breasted, to alternate with the double-breasted blue Chesterfield for special occasions.

I would also recommend a pair of formal flannel trousers for extra leg warmth and that any woolen garments should contain no less than 400 to 480 grams of wool. Don't be afraid to allow for dashes of colour and a sense of fun in your selections too. Be versatile and go for a mix of double and single-breasted styles, pinstripes, browns and greens. Plump for tweed or velvet for your sports jacket as they work well on a day in the country or at the races."

What about spring and autumn?
DP: "As spring and autumn can be similar, two fabrics are essential here – gabardine and solaro. The former is quite hard to work with and will really put the tailor's skills to the test. In fact, there are few tailors left who can work with it. Solaro, on the other hand, is more for everyday use. Apart from these two, any other fabric can be worn provided it is no thicker than 300 to 320 grams per metre."

And what if we have an unseasonably cold snap in spring or autumn?
DP: "Overcoats should be waterproof and single-breasted with hidden brown buttons. Known as

cover coats, they are characterised by four seams on each cuff. As for the traditional raincoat, it need not be handmade as it won't get much use in Italy."

What about formal wear for special occasions like gala evenings or an opening night at La Scala?
DP: "A well-dressed gent will be equally well-armed for this kind of occasion, no matter what the weather outside, be it with a heavy or light garment, close or loose fitting – not forgetting the staple tailcoat and black-tie suit (or tuxedo). Flannel fabric will avoid any creasing. In days gone by, before industrialised fabrics came along, we wore flannel and flannel only."

How do we deal with the heat of summer?
DP: "Early July to mid-September is the season for linens, cottons and mohair. Here again the more you have in your wardrobe, the better. Double or single-breasted, crushed or not."

Why do you tend towards "the more the better"?
DP: "The reason is simple. Clothes 'live' and if we wear them too often then they 'fall ill' and get out of shape. They are delicate and need to be cared for and rested. Wear an item one day; let it rest for four. That's how to get the best out of your wardrobe."

Is the same true of shoes?
DP: "Indeed. Wear them one day then leave the shoetree in them the next. So, ideally you need ten or so pairs. Opt for a variety of styles, from brown Derby brogues to 'Norwegian' styles for those long walks in the winter countryside, with double buckles for a touch of extravagance."

So finally we come to shirts…
DP: "A smart gent should have at least 12 of the following – white, blue, striped and linen. Nowadays we tend to only change clothes twice a day at the most, whereas in the past gentlemen would easily change four or five times a day. They'd wear something light in the morning, something darker in the afternoon, then darker still in the evening before perhaps another change for the theatre or dinner."

How important should a gentleman's wardrobe be to him?
DP: "What he wears is a reflection of his inner self. To get an understanding of the man who stands before you, you only need to study his clothes. You'll grasp something of who he is and whether he has class."

ENGLISH ETIQUETTE AND DEPENDABLE DECORUM

WILL SUTTON

To quote Sir Patrick Moore: "The height of Englishness is good manners." Whether strolling through the side streets of Kensington or rambling across The Hangers Way in Hampshire, a true English gent would stand between the road and his lady or lift a branch for her to pass under. Over the past 100 years, our idea of what an English gentleman should be has not altered too much, albeit that today he sports the ubiquitous mobile phone and sunglasses. However, the need for a well-fitted suit, closely shaven beard, and impeccable manners and politeness still stand.

Some may argue that the rise of the independent woman in society should shift things along. Who should now foot the bill? Traditionally, the man as the main breadwinner was financially responsible for the family unit. Modern Western society may not be altogether unanimous on the issue, but good manners cost nothing and define our notion of acceptable social behaviour nevertheless.

Here are some of the most commonly accepted rules of behaviour:

- Eye contact during conversation as it indicates that you're interested and engaged in the other's story
- Similarly, when engaged in conversation, take your hands out of your pockets
- Do not over-squeeze someone's hand during a handshake, but worse still is a limp handshake. It lacks any sort of character whatsoever
- Hold the door open for others and, just as importantly, when riding on public transport always offer your seat to an elderly person or pregnant woman. Some would add that if a carriage is packed and only one seat remains, for example, you should really give your seat up to a lady standing
- During professional exchanges, it is deemed correct to receive a business card with two hands and look at the card upon receipt. Remarking on the card itself, if it is particularly unusual, is a bonus
- Never be afraid to apologise when an apology is warranted. There is nothing ruder than a person who never says sorry for bad or sloppy behaviour, such as lateness, lack of thought, taking credit for something when it's clearly not yours to take
- Avoid talking loudly in public or especially on your phone – the latter is widely perceived as "showing off" and there's no excuse for it.

- Never start to read or write text messages when a person is talking to you – that too is one of the rudest things you could do.

Dinner party etiquette is another ball game. There are many formalities to take into consideration when arranging a dinner party. The host should ensure the table is correctly laid well ahead of time. The menu should reflect the season – light food for summer, comforting foods for winter. Aperitifs are essential – wine or cocktails, and soft drinks and juices for non-drinkers. Most importantly, guests should be given enough time to enjoy at least two aperitifs. Moving on to seating and order of service, the female guest of honour should sit to the host's right and should always be served first. Dishes are then passed anti-clockwise. Every dish served should be done so with the relevant silverware and the guest should only commence eating upon direction from the host. Male guests should not remove their jackets until the host has done so; the same goes for being seated. Gentle humour can be good for breaking the ice among groups of strangers.

Above all else there are two unwritten rules that should be observed at every dining occasion:

1   Women should never have to pour their own wine
2   When port is presented – usually alongside the cheese board and in a decanter – it is always passed to the left; pour a glass for your fellow guest on the right before doing so.

Sticking to these social graces at a dinner party should ensure that you receive future invitations, but also that you maintain an air of dignity and social standing. Beyond all, regardless of the hangover the following day, always write to thank the host for the evening.

THE GOLDEN AGE OF ITALIAN TAILORING

DANIELA MONTALBANO

"Beauty is the greatest gift granted to man by God as thanks to beauty we can raise our spirit to contemplation." Angelo Firenzuola, 1578

Authentic Italian tailoring is alive and well in the 21st century. The tradition of handmade clothing has been a part of Italy's cultural heritage for many centuries, lending Italian men their inimitable sense of style. The key to this successful tradition lies in the close relationship between tailor and client, in which every little detail can be recorded from posture to gait.

Each stage of the tailoring process is carried out with great dexterity, and you can't help but marvel at the cutting techniques that combine with basting, stitching and subsequent streaking, not to mention the understanding of materials to ensure the correct approach at all times.

Clients from around the world travel to cities like Naples, Milan and Florence for a share of Italian craftsmanship. Milan may be the seat of forward-thinking fashion, but elsewhere in Italy bespoke tailoring is also a national art that requires attention to detail, an accurate choice of materials and meticulous manufacturing. Think woven fabrics, hand-embroidered eyelets, mother-of-pearl buttons and silk stitching.

Stepping into a tailor's studio is a wonderful exercise in nostalgia; sewing needles, scissors and tape measures scattered all around, and with the comforting smell of the steam iron used to shape, moisten and stretch the fabric.

The tailor is a creative director, who will overlook every stage of production on every type of unique garment, from tight-waisted jackets to low-waisted trousers with diagonally-cut trouser pockets that slim the silhouette. Colours can be as vivid and bright as a summer's day, or smart and formal with elegant greys and sleek dark tones.

Baroque Neapolitan garments are a triumph of curved lines and architectural boldness that date back to the small family workshops of yesteryear. Sartorial excellence is taken very seriously here in the south of Italy, with the Neapolitan Giacca and the shirt-style shoulder (spalla camicia) that eschews the use of shoulder pads. While the Dandy Giacca

→ 1. HAND STITCHING PROCESS OF SUIT BY N H SARTORIA

style bucks the trend with eccentric and relaxed pieces, outlined in soft unstructured shapes and balanced by well-defined shoulders pads.

For those passionate about Italian bespoke tailoring, but who can't travel, there is now an online service, called Net Tailor, which uses technology to detect a client's measurements, body shape and posture – just as you'd expect from the sartorially savvy Italians.

THE RIGHT TUXEDO IS
A MATTER OF TIMING

SARA CASTILLO ROMERO

The black-tie outfit is the ultimate mark of elegance and class in a man's wardrobe.

Henry Poole & Co was commissioned to make a dinner jacket for the Prince of Wales, later Edward VII, to wear to informal parties and, by 1885, he was sporting this Savile Row "tailless" suit to all his informal outings. In the spring of 1886, the prince invited American James Potter to Sandringham for a spot of hunting. It was when Potter asked for the dress code for dinner that the Prince of Wales advised him to visit Henry Poole & Co for some sartorial assistance. When Potter returned home to New York, his London jacket proved to be something of a hit at the Tuxedo Park Club, a society for wealthy individuals who shared a love of hunting and fishing in the Tuxedo area. From that moment on, the British black-tie suit was dubbed the "tuxedo" by North Americans, while Europeans would refer to it as "The Smoking", wearing it when they would inevitably have to step outside for their cigarette breaks at parties.

A great deal of the black tie's success can be attributed to the British Royal Family. Edward VII had conceived of the tailless jacket, while his grandson, the Duke of Winsor, was frequently seen stepping out in his black-tie suit to attend glamorous evening events.

The Hollywood film industry swiftly followed, establishing the "tuxedo protocol" at award evenings and film premieres as the great stars of the silver screen boosted its worldwide appeal. The Oscar-winning film, The Artist, showcased the black tie or tuxedo as a 20th-century men's classic through the telling lens of French director Michel Hazanavicius.

Far from remaining exclusively black, there have been varyingly unsuccessful attempts at colour introduced throughout the decades, notably with the Duke of Windsor who preferred his jackets dark blue. There were some more questionable attempts by others in the 1960s and '70s to bring colour to the black tie (think lilac, red and yellow). These would probably be best forgotten now, but at the time they were deemed cutting-edge.

In Victorian and Edwardian times, a black tie was in fact only used for informal occasions and in contrast the white tie was worn to gentlemen's meetings held after 6pm or in female company. Between the wars, the white tie was increasingly favoured for formal functions, such as balls or fundraising dinners, while the black tie was reserved for evening wear. Cole Porter and Noel Coward were great ambassadors in the 1930s, and in the '40s and the '50s the black tie took on more formality

→ 1. ILLUSTRATION BY ARTURO ELENA *www.arturoelena.com*

for dinner parties, immortalised by the likes of Frank Sinatra and Dean Martin. After a slight decline in the '60s and '70s, it made a dramatic comeback in the booming '80s and is now most famously associated with the iconic James Bond. Unfortunately, nowadays the dress code is less obvious unless stated, although prestigious occasions, like the ballet or the opera, still require a black-tie dress code (the Dress Circle derives its name from it).

How to wear a tuxedo

Generally, there are a number of guidelines for how a tuxedo should look:

1 Black or midnight-blue cloth – often barathea or plain cloth, sometimes with a touch of mohair for an elegant sheen
2 Classic options are peaked lapels covered in black silk satin, repp or moiré with a single button or a double-breasted front; or a shawl collar with black silk and single button closure
3 Ventless jacket

4   Cummerbund or waistcoat with a single-button jacket
5   Neither a cummerbund nor a waistcoat should be worn with a double-breasted jacket and
    the waist must never be exposed
6   Wear braces (suspenders in the US) – never a belt
7   A galon stripe on the side of the trousers
8   Jetted pockets – no flaps, because these are considered to be informal
9   Pocket square – traditionally in white linen, but a splash of colour in silk or linen is just
    as good
10 White or ivory shirts with double cuffs and a turndown collar with pleats, and starched,
    marcella piqué front or a fly front if no studs are available
11 Black silk bow tie matching the lapel
12 A boutonniere in the lapel –a highly overlooked but great finishing detail
13 Black over-the-calf socks made of pure silk
14 Black patent leather Oxford shoes (without a captoe/brogues) or plain opera pumps.

In his book Dressing the Man, classic couturier Alan Flusher provides wise advice on the
benefits of discretion when choosing a fabric finish: "Like the tailcoat, dinner clothes are
trimmed in facings of varying degrees of luster; therefore, so as not to overstate the sheen
quotient, the dinner jacket's base cloth should be in a dulled or matte finish. Subtle textured
weave effects, such as baratheas and mini-herringbones or quiet variegated effects, avoid
affectation while adding surface interest to the formal ensemble."

In the modern style-conscious fashion world, the stately tuxedo has been reinvigorated as
young men opt for colour and bold tailoring. Fashion designers, obsessed as they are these days
with all manner of tailored clothing, have been busy reinventing the tux. It is now said that
"the traditional tuxedo has given way to a more 'interpretive' dress code". Goodbye, black tie.
But the purpose of formalwear is to show honour and respect no matter what the occasion.

Every man should at least learn the traditional rules of formal evening wear and then have the
freedom to add their own personal style. Or as the Los Angeles Times put it: The right wedding
tuxedo is a matter of timing. And as Mr Armani noted, the tuxedo "will always be the gold
standard" – there are enough options in formalwear to express individuality without discarding
the basic concept.

→ 2. ILLUSTRATION BY ARTURO ELENA *www.arturoelena.com*

THE SHAVE OF
YOUR LIFE

RAOUL KEIL & HUMA HUMAYUN

There was a time, not so long ago, when the idea of looking well-groomed was considered… well… not so manly. Carefully dishevelled hair, which in fairness, probably took the best part of an hour to arrange, and a quick going over with a Bic razor were all that were required for the cool cats of East London. But now, a new aesthetic is taking over Old Street and its environs. Wet shaves are all the rage as traditional barber shops spring up around the capital.

When I say "traditional" barber shop, I don't mean the kind of place where you can get a short back and sides for small change or choose a haircut from the faded posters in the window. No, now we're talking retro-chic interiors, luxury products from the likes of Acqua di Genova and Czech & Speake, with an optional facial and a locally brewed beer – or even a malt whisky – on the side.

So, why the increasing interest in our furry follicles? It has been suggested that the groomed look took off because of the hit TV series Mad Men and its meticulously clean-shaven cast. Beards are back in vogue thanks to Brad Pitt, Jude Law and Johnny Depp, while the success of men's health charity Movember has seen moustaches lose their Burt Reynolds-style seedy '70s connotations. Certainly nostalgia for old-fashioned quality and a more put-together look seems to be prevalent in men's fashion in general.

The idea of a gentleman shaving himself at home is a fairly new one. A trip to the "penny barber" for a wet shave was a weekly routine for the average bloke, while a gentleman would be shaved at home by a manservant. Now, changeable blades have brought life back to this ancient ritual. Barbers date back to the Bronze Age and, from medieval times, often doubled up as surgeons or dentists. The red-and-white striped pole outside was used to dry bloody bandages. Well, you don't get much manlier than that.

However, if you're looking for a grooming experience that is more St James's than Sweeney Todd, London has much to offer, both in terms of new establishments, and those that have been wafting hot and cold towels and wielding cut-throat razors long before a moustache was just for Movember. The Pall Mall Barbers has been catering to its central-London clientele since 1896 and uses handmade products from the 200-year-old D.R. Harris pharmacy nearby. A popular newcomer is Murdock London, which opened in Shoreditch in 2006 and already has three more stores around the capital. It offers a "how to shave" tutorial as well

→ 1. PHOTOGRAPHY - JACK WATERLOT

as a luxury service including shampoo and haircut, wet shave, facial, head massage and a manicure or shoe-shine.

Retailers have also cottoned on to the idea that men crave a bit of sanctuary from the shopping experience. Top Man, Ben Sherman and Ted Baker now all offer in-store barbers. Murdoch's Grooming, located in Liberty, provides facials and manicures as well as haircuts and wet shaves, with a focus on artisanal products. A selection of vintage books and magazines is also on hand to help while away the "me" time.

A large part of the appeal of these establishments is the decidedly masculine environment. Men are hankering after a pampering that doesn't involve a noisy unisex salon drowning in the sound of hairdryers, Capital FM and the obligatory "Been on holiday lately?" chit-chat. Away from the constant onslaught of the digital age, the barber's shop is a place to take time out and indulge in one of the few luxuries in life that is still strictly for men only. It certainly beats a Yorkie bar.

DIRECTORY

ALFRED DUNHILL

- ALFRED DUNHILL

5-7 Mandeville Place
London, W1U 3AY
+44 (0) 20 7838 8000
www.dunhill.co.uk

- ARCHER ADAMS

2 Chiltern Street,
London W1U 7P4
+44 (0) 207 935 3582
www.archeradams.com
reception@archeradams.com

- ASPINAL OF LONDON

Aspinal House,
Longfield, Fernhurst,
West Sussex, GU29 3HA
0808 1443302
www.aspinaloflondon.com
enquiries@aspinaloflondon.com

RICCARDO FRECCIA BESTETTI
CALZATURE ARTIGIANALI

- RICCARDO FRECCIA BESTETTI

via Manara Negrone 32/R
27029 Vigevano - Italy
www.frecciabestetti.com
rfbestetti@gmail.com
frecciabestetti@frecciabestetti.com

- CAD AND THE DANDY

First Floor
13 Savile Row
London, W1S 3NE
0207 283 1975
www.cadandthedandy.co.uk
info@cadandthedandy.co.uk

JOSEPH
CHEANEY
& SONS

- CHEANEY SHOES - FLAGSHIP SHOP

4 Piccadilly Arcade,
St James's
London, SW1Y 6NH
+44 (0) 20 7495 6413
www.cheaney.co.uk

- CHEANEY SHOES - Factory location

69 Rushton Road,
Desborough
Northamptonshire. NN14 2RR
+44 (0)1536 760383

- DALMORE

John Stevenson
Head of VIP Client Relations
+44 (0) 777 552 1704
John.stevenson@thedalmore.com

- DASHING TWEEDS

5 St. Mark's Crescent,
London NW1 7TS
Tel.:+44 (0)20 7267 3352
www.DashingTweeds.co.uk

- DEGE & SKINNER

10 Savile Row
London, W1S 3PF
+44 (0) 207 287 2941
www.dege-skinner.co.uk
enquiries@dege-skinner.co.uk

- DENTS

Furnax Lane, Warminster
Wiltshire, UK, BA12 8PE
+44 (0) 1985 212291
www.dents.co.uk
dents@dents.co.uk

- ETTINGER

215 Putney Bridge Road
London. SW15 2NY, UK
+44 (0)20 8877 1616
www.ettinger.co.uk

- FIELDING & NICHOLSON

+44 (0) 207 324 6049
www.fieldingandnicholson.com
team@fieldingandnicholson.com

• GIEVES & HAWKES

No.1 Savile Row
London, W1S 3JR
020 7432 6403

www.gievesandhawkes.com

Mr.Hare

• MR. HARE

8 Stafford St
Mayfair
London, W1S 4RU
+44 (0) 207 495 4200

www.mrhare.com

ESTABLISHED 1806
HENRY POOLE & CO
15 SAVILE ROW, LONDON W1S 3PJ

• HENRY POOLE & CO *(Savile Row)* LTD

15 Savile Row
London, W1S 3PJ
+44 (0) 20 7734 5985

www.henrypoole.com

HOLLAND & HOLLAND
Established London 1835

• HOLLAND & HOLLAND

JOHN STEVENSON
Head of VIP Client Relations
Direct + 44 (0) 777 552 1704
Switchboard + 44 (0) 207 499 4411
33 Bruton Street. Mayfair. London W1J 6HH
John.stevenson@hollandandholland.com

JAEGER

• JAEGER

+ 44 (0) 845 521 0495
www.jaeger.co.uk

JIMMY CHOO

• JIMMY CHOO

JIMMY CHOO MEN'S BOUTIQUES
London, 35 Dover Street, +44 (0)20 7495 7195 (May 2013)
Hong Kong, Elements Kowloon, +852 2196 8966
Tokyo, Hankyu, +81 3 6252 5323
Osaka, Hankyu, +81 80 1227 0134
www.jimmychoo.com

• JUST BLAZE

+ 44 (0) 7539924630
www.dvobello.com
ok@dvobello.com

• KILGOUR

No.8 Savile Row
London, W1S 3PE
+ 44 (0) 800 953 5841

customerservices@kilgour.com

• LINKS OF LONDON

Flagship Store
16 Sloane Square
London, SW1W 8ER

www.linksoflondon.com

• MULBERRY

50 New Bond Street
London , W1S 1BJ
+44 (0) 20 7491 3900

• MURDOCK LONDON

18 Monmouth Street,
London, WC2H 9HB
+44 (0) 203 393 7946

www.murdocklondon.com

• N.H SARTORIA

Via Chiossetto, 2 - 20122 Milano
Tel +39 02 780 531
Mob +39 335 6092902

info@nhsartoria.it
www.nhsartoria.it

OLIVER PEOPLES

• OLIVER PEOPLES

812 Madison Ave
New York, NY 10065
212-585-3433

www.oliverpeoples.com

• PASSAGGIO CRAVATTE

+39 339 470 31 56
+39 339 222 78 88

www.passaggiocravatte.com
info@passaggiocravatte.com

Paul Smith

- PAUL SMITH
  - **PAUL SMITH FAUBOURG ST HONORE**
  3 Rue du Faubourg St Honore
  Paris, 75008, France
  +33 1 42 68 27 10

  - **PAUL SMITH GREENE STREET**
  142 Greene Street
  New York, NY 10012, United States
  +1 646 613 3060

  - **PAUL SMITH No. 9 ALBEMARLE STREET**
  Opening August 2013
  9 Albemarle Street
  Mayfair, London, W1S 4HH, United Kingdom
  www.paulsmith.co.uk

Paul Smith
BESPOKE

- PAUL SMITH WESTBOURNE HOUSE
  122 Kensington Park Road
  Notting Hill
  London, W11 2EP
  United Kingdom
  +44 020 7727 3553
  www.paulsmith.co.uk

RALPH LAUREN

- RALPH LAUREN
  No. 1 New Bond Street
  London, W1S 3RL,
  +44 0207 535 4600

  105-109 Fulham Road
  London, SW3 6SD,
  +44 0207 590 7990

  Double RL, 16 Mount Street
  London, W1K 2RH,
  +44 0207 953 4120

  208 Ingram Street
  Glasgow, G1 1DQ
  www.ralphlauren.com

MAKERS OF THE FINEST SHOTGUNS AND RIFLES

- RAY WARD
  12 Cadogan Place
  Knightsbridge
  London, SW1X 9PU
  +44 (0) 800 953 5844
  customerservices@rayward.co.uk

- SHARP & DAPPER
  +44 (0)7790653264
  www.sharpanddapper.com

ESTABLISHED 1806
HENRY POOLE & CO

• SHAW SPEED & CUSTOM

Holmes Hill, Near Lewes
East Sussex, BN8 6JA
Tel 01825 872003
Fax 01825 874319
www.shawspeedandcustom.co.uk
stevew@shawspeedandcustom.co.uk

TED BAKER
LONDON

• TED BAKER

- REGENT STREET
245 Regent Street
London, W1B 2EN, UK
+44 (0) 20 7493 6251

- FLORAL STREET
9 -10 Floral Street
Covent Garden
London, WC2E 9HW, UK
+44 (0) 20 7836 7808

- KNIGHTSBRIDGE
75 Brompton Road, Knightsbridge
London, SW3 1DB, UK
+44 (0) 20 7589 5399
www.tedbaker.com

• VILLA

Via Manzoni 23
20121 Milano
+39 02 804279
www.villa.it
info@villa.it

ADDITIONAL EDITORIAL & IMAGE CONTRIBUTORS

BRIAN GRAINGER	Translator graingerbri@gmail.com
NATHALIE GRAINGER BRADBURY	Content editor, copy writer and translator graingernathalie@yahoo.co.uk
FRANÇOIS BOUTEMY	Photographer - Cheaney Shoes www.simulacrastudio.com
SARA CASTILLO ROMERO	Quintessentially Creative Project Manager, +44 (0) 7788 480 058 www.quintessentiallycreative.com - Sara.romero@quintessentially.com
GIANNI CERUTTI	Luxury lifestyle journalist and founder of Passaggio Cravatte www.passaggiocravatte.com - cerutti.gianni@gmail.com
GIORGIO CRISCIONE	Designer and Illustrator www.giorgiocriscione.com
HUMA HUMAYUN	Features & Fashion Editor, Schön! Magazine www.schonmagazine.com
RAOUL KEIL	Editor-inChief, Schön! Magazine www.schonmagazine.com
DANIELA MONTALBANO	Fashion Stylist, Art Buyer and Make-up Artist www.dmdaniela.com - info@dmdaniela.com
JAMES SHERWOOD	Author, Broadcaster and Curator www.james-sherwood.com - james@james-sherwood.com
WILL SUTTON	Lifestyle Editor, +44 (0) 7731 465 381 wrcsutton@gmail.com

ACKNOWLEGEMENTS

Q GENTLEMAN PROJECT MANAGER • Will Sutton

HEAD OF PRODUCTION • Lois Crompton

DESIGN • Giorgio Criscione
and Chris Charalambous

CREATOR OF SKETCH ILLUSTRATIONS *(except Jimmy Choo)* • Giorgio Criscione

HEAD OF EDITORIAL AND WRITER • Nathalie Bradbury

TOP EDITOR • Peter Archer

EDITORIAL ASSISTANCE • Michael Hurley,
Hilary Burns,
Angela Stobaugh
and Alicia Martinenko

CEO OF QCREATIVE • Rebecca Tucker

OUR PRINTERS IN ITALY • EBS

*Thank you also to all of our participating houses whose
content and images animate our book to stunning effect.*

Quintessentially Publishing Ltd.
29 Portland Place, London, W1B 1QB
Tel +44 (0)20 3073 6845
info@quintessentiallypublishing.com
www.quintessentiallypublishing.com

No part of this book may be reproduced or transmitted
electronically or mechanically, including photocopying
without permission of the publisher.

Copyright 2013
Quintessentially Publishing Ltd.
All rights reserved

ISBN: 978-0-9569952-7-8

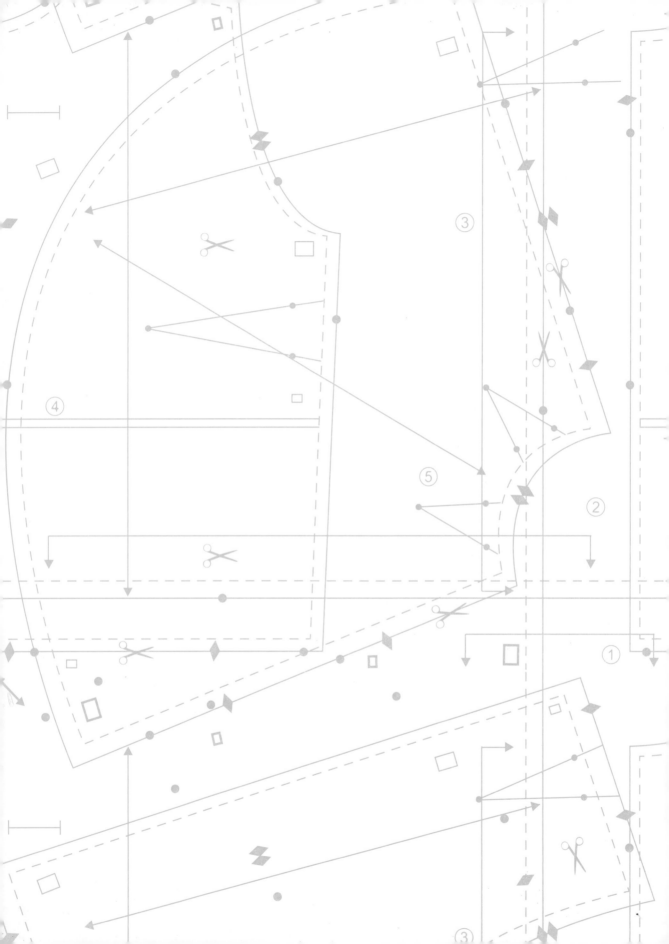